R. D. Bartlett and Patricia P. Bartlett

Anoles, Basilisks, and Water Dragons

Everything About Selection, Care, Nutrition, Breeding, and Behavior

Filled with Full-color Photographs
Illustrations by Michele Earle-Bridges

BARRON'S

CONTENTS

3

Although they are not closely related and vary widely in size, anoles, basilisks, and water dragons require much the same regimen of care to thrive in captivity. Spacious cages, access to sunlight or ultraviolet lighting, and a healthy diet are the basics of good care.

Guidelines for All

The anoles, basilisks, and water dragons (including the sail-tailed dragons) are dissimilar lizards with many similar husbandry needs. All are lizards of subtropical and tropical settings (with a range extending to North Carolina and southeastern Oklahoma, the green anole is by far the most northerly species). Collectively they are creatures of forests, savannas, and riparian settings. The anoles and basilisks are of New World distribution and the water dragons are creatures of the Old World. The basilisks and the water dragons are bipedal runners, strong swimmers, and have a laterally compressed tail. Three of the four basilisk species and the sail-tailed dragons have prominently fringed toes. A few anoles frequent stream

Adult green water dragons may sit for long periods with an alert, heads-up posture.

edges and plunge into the water and hide beneath submerged rocks and debris to escape predators. Although these anoles don't hesitate to enter the water, they are not particularly strong swimmers.

The anoles are the smallest members of this lizard triad, the basilisks and water dragons of the genus *Physignathus* are the next largest, and the sail-tailed dragons (genus *Hydrosaurus*) are the largest of all.

There are many reasons why these lizards have caught the fancy of hobbyists. The anoles are of interest because of the color changing ability of many species and because of the climbing ability of most. (Only the geckos exceed the anoles in their ability to climb smooth vertical surfaces including glass.) The ability of three of the four basilisk species to run rapidly across the surface of quiet water when startled and the amazing crests seen on the males of two species keep these lizards in the herpetocultural forefront. Although the water dragons are less adept than the anoles and basilisks in climbing and are unable to run across the water's surface, they are nicely colored, have well-developed serrate vertebral crests, and with their pug-nosed countenance, are just plain cute. The sail-tailed dragons, big bruisers when adult, are the least commonly seen members of this group. Adult males bear tall crests on their tails.

Because of the large size of the basilisks and water dragons and the constraints of most cages, it will be difficult to observe any but the most cursory of aspects of even quasi-natural behavior in captivity. Certainly these lizards will feed, drink, bask, sleep, climb, and perhaps, breed, but they will be unable to indulge in their typical bipedal running, powerful swimming, or to regale you with their ability to run across the surface of water.

However, in a properly appointed cage of reasonable size, the small size and rather quiet demeanor of most anoles will allow at least a naturalistic approach to life. Not only will anoles feed, drink, bask, sleep, and breed, but if they are provided with limbs of the proper diameter and with foliage the little lizards are quite apt to display their ability to pursue and catch food insects in the leaves and they will quickly scurry around to the far side of a limb and hide at your approach. During the spring and summer breeding season male anoles will often bob their head, indulge in pushups, and repeatedly distend their dewlap. These territoriality displays are apt to be especially emphatic if two males can temporarily see each other. However, lengthy visual contact even between adjacent terraria will cause undue and unwanted stress.

Stress

Many hobbyists—and not only novice hobbyists—attempt to maintain too many lizards in either too small, or incorrectly appointed, terraria. The result for the lizards is stress.

Stress does not have to be particularly overt or dramatic to prove eventually lethal to your lizards.

Some examples of stressful situations are:
• insufficient visual barriers
• too small a caging facility
• adverse extraneous stimuli
• aggression toward subordinates by dominant lizards.

The first three are easily recognizable to virtually all keepers, and they can be corrected by, respectively, the placement of additional visual barriers (such as plantings, limbs, etc.), by providing larger caging facilities or reducing the number of lizards in the present one, and by either taping an opaque shield over the glass or by moving the cage of nervous lizards into a less heavily trafficked area. On the other hand, recognizing intraspecific aggression (dominance) is not always so easy, but it is every bit as critical as the more readily determined kinds of stress.

Intraspecific aggression by these lizards can sometimes, but not always, involve actual physical conflict. The aggression can be much more subtle, yet every bit as potentially lethal. Such normal behavior by a dominant lizard as the claiming of the best basking perch, the nodding of the head, the flaring of the dewlap, or an intensification of body color—all done without actual physical contact—can and will cause a reduction in the feeding and other responses of subordinate lizards. Males usually (but not always) interact adversely with other males, and females with other females. The larger the cage, the fewer the lizards of a single species, and the greater the number of visual barriers, the less critical these interactions may be. Be advised, however, that these interactions can and will occur, and they can—and eventually will—take their toll.

Strange, and often not understood by the casual hobbyist, is how the presence of two males of a given species in a large cage can be debilitating when those two lizards were chosen from among a dozen lizards that were housed, apparently peacefully, in a tiny cage at a pet dealer. The difference is that the chaos in that dealer's small tank was so great that it was impossible for any of the lizards to display any normal actions and reactions, including territoriality. It is probable that eventually the stress caused by such a situation would have been fatal to all but the strongest male and, possibly, female lizard. However, when removed from that chaos to the quasi-normalcy of an appropriate cage, the natural instincts of the lizards are again possible and are activated. Territory as well as dominance is quickly established. Lizards that appeared to have been equals in the dealer's cage become subordinates, and the stress can be channeled. A rather good rule of thumb is to house only one male and two or three females of a given species in any single cage, no matter how large. In most cases, such a group will thrive.

Arm Waving

The water and the sail-tailed dragons utilize a method of arm waving (an appeasement motion) called circumduction. It is used in communicating with others of their own species. Circumduction is nothing more than a circular waving motion of a front limb, palm outward,

and directed toward the other lizard. The motion apparently appeases dominant and/or aggressive agamids toward their subordinates and is useful in establishing hierarchical positions. Circumduction is most evident in subordinate females but is not uncommonly used by hatchlings and juveniles, apparently of both sexes.

Shedding

Like snakes, as lizards grow, they periodically shed their outer skin. However, unlike snakes, which, if healthy and kept in healthy conditions, usually shed in a single, unbroken piece, the skin of most lizards (and of all of those discussed in this book) is shed in "patchwork" fashion. This is entirely normal and does not indicate an underlying problem.

Lizards shed their skin most frequently during periods of rapid growth or following injury or skin disorders. This, too, is natural, normal, and necessary.

Expect baby lizards to shed their skin more frequently than adults, and those that eat well to shed more frequently than those that don't. Lizards of all sizes shed soon after emerging from hibernation.

The Phenomenon of Natural Sunlight

Ultraviolet-A (UV-A) and ultraviolet-B (UV-B) are known to be important stimulants to lizards and are integral to lizard behavior. Both are amply provided by natural, unfiltered sunlight; even the best reptile sunning bulbs available don't compare to the benefits of natural sunlight.

The Hispaniolan green anole, Anolis chlorocyanus, *is tenuously established in southeastern Florida.*

UV-A stimulates "natural behavior" in a lizard (or other reptile). Apparently, different strengths of UV-A stimulate differing behavior patterns, with that induced by full-strength, unfiltered sunlight being the most natural.

Is this good? Is "natural behavior" what you really want for your lizard?

Well, certainly, natural behavior is the best for a lizard. Heliothermic lizards are adapted to bask in and utilize the various rays of natural sunlight. It is under this regimen that lizards are the most alert, the most apt to breed, the best able to avoid danger, and the best able to defend themselves if caught unsuspectingly.

All of these factors seem to be impaired, at least to a small degree, when heliothermic lizards are denied access to full-strength, unfiltered, natural sunlight.

How do we know this? Well, simply approach—or try to approach—a green water

A young adult male Weber's sail-tailed dragon.

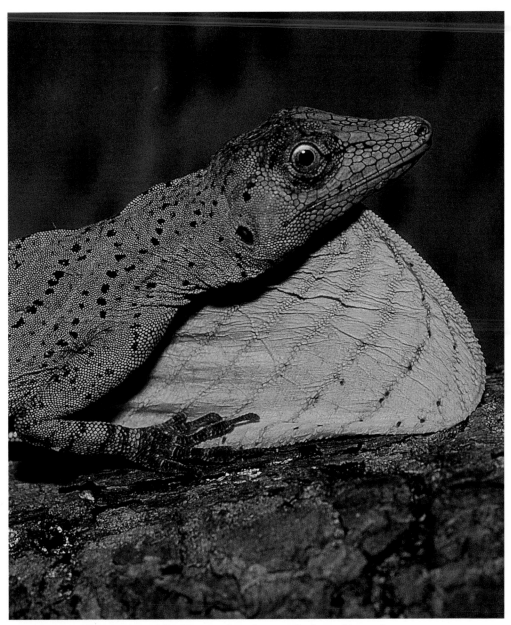

The bright yellow dewlap of the blue-eyed anole extends from chin to chest.

dragon in the wild. Most often, the lizard will see you long before you see it, and the only indication you'll have of its whereabouts is a thrashing in the underbrush or a splash followed by a series of ripples in a water hole. But if you had approached and caught that lizard, you would have been bitten, scratched, and tail-whipped. This is natural behavior. For a day or two after the lizard has been taken captive, the same behavior is seen, but after a week or so, the lizard's responses become dull.

It no longer darts away when it is approached, and it is infinitely easier to handle when you choose to do so. "So what?" you ask. "The lizard is just getting tame. And, after all, that's exactly what we want." "Tame" lizards tend not to smash their noses up in mad dashes for freedom, nor do they rip you, the handler, to shreds.

But is your lizard truly tame?

Put that tame lizard out into the unfiltered sunlight for a day—an hour, for that matter—and watch its reversion to a truly natural behavior. It will dart away when approached, it will bite, scratch, and whip you when caught, and it will be, in every way, a wild lizard again.

If you were to leave that same lizard outside in the sunlight, but with a pane of UV-filtering glass between it and the sun (taking care not to cook the lizard!), within a day or two, you'd again have a docile lizard.

Similar experiments, obliterating just the UV-A, have produced similar results.

This does not mean that you cannot tame a lizard. It just means that not all lizards that you think are tame actually are, and that you should not be surprised at behavioral changes induced by natural, unfiltered sunlight.

What happens when UV-B is removed? We have now learned that when reptiles, which syn-thesize vitamin D_3 in their skin, are denied access to UV-B, the synthesis of this important vitamin stops. The production of D_3 is of paramount importance, for in reptiles D_3 is a calcium metabolizer. Lack of D_3 equates to an inability to metabolize calcium, even when ample calcium is present in the diet. The end result of this is the onset of metabolic bone disease. Thus, captive heliothermic (sun-basking) lizards will need both exposure to UV-A and UV-B, as well as dietary D_3 supplementation.

Hormonally Stimulated Aggression

Lizards of all species are least aggressive during non-breeding periods and when they are severely stressed. Conversely, they are most aggressive when temperatures and photoperiods dictate the advent of the breeding seasons and when they have established a territory. Males are almost invariably more territorial (at least in this grouping of lizards), hence more aggressive than females. Although aggressive behavior is largely intraspecific (same species) in the wild, lizards in captivity occasionally direct aggression at very dissimilar objects. You, as your lizard's keeper, can become one of these dissimilar objects, and can become the target of aggression.

Of course, with lizards as small as most anoles, aggression would be of small concern; even for a water dragon, a sudden display of aggressive behavior is more startling than dangerous. But, to have a lizard that was readily handled a day earlier suddenly confront a reaching hand with gaping jaws and whipping tail concerns some keepers. This behavior, too, shall pass as the breeding season ends.

Where and How to Find Anoles, Basilisks, and Water Dragons in the United States

Green Anole: Look for this abundant species in sun-drenched trees and shrubs, on fences and porches, and in other elevated habitats from northern North Carolina to southeastern Oklahoma and eastern Texas.

Pale-throated Green Anole: Individuals with light gray to off-white throats may occur from Sarasota County to Miami-Dade County, Florida. Trees (including those that have fallen), shrubs, fences, and buildings are among the habitats utilized by this lizard.

Brown Anole: This now ubiquitous lizard is found throughout Florida and much of Hawaii, in some coastal areas of southern Georgia, and occurs in isolated populations in southern Alabama, Louisiana, and Texas.

Knight Anole: This huge anole may be seen in the canopy (cold weather) and on lower trunks (hot weather) of large ornamental trees. It especially favors introduced figs (*Ficus*). Although it is most common in Miami-Dade County, it also occurs sparingly in southern Broward County, Monroe County, and Collier County, Florida.

Bark Anole: This small anole may be most reliably found in city and county parks and treed industrial complexes in Miami-Dade and Monroe counties, FL. It is often 3 to 6 feet off the ground in a head-down position on small- to medium-sized trees.

Large-headed Anole: This is an uncommon anole. It is most often seen positioned in a head down position rather low on the trunks of large trees in greater Miami and Miami-Dade County.

Hispaniolan Green Anole: This uncommon and very locally-distributed anole may be found on shade trees in some parts of Miami, and Miami-Dade County.

Cuban Green Anole: This increasingly common and very arboreal species is very similar in appearance to the native green anole. The Cuban green anole may be most reliably found on trees in city and county parks and other treed areas in Miami-Dade and Monroe counties, FL.

Crested Anole: This brownish anole is most abundant in the greater Miami area and Miami-Dade County. It may be seen on fences, in piles of limestone rubble or construction debris, low on tree trunks, and on low walls.

Jamaican Giant Anole: This very arboreal anole is found both in the canopy and on the upper trunks of shade trees in a few areas in Miami-Dade County.

Basilisks: Of the four species, only the northern brown basilisk is firmly established. Look for this large lizard along the banks of quiet ponds and canals in the greater Miami area. It is very common in many city and county parks.

Water Dragons: None are yet established in the USA.

ACQUIRING YOUR LIZARDS

Keeping anoles, basilisks, water dragons, or their relatives in captivity over a long period of time is a lot easier if you begin your adventure with healthy specimens. We offer you some suggestions to help you choose.

Choosing a Healthy Specimen

• Choose a lizard with a plump body and fleshy pelvic area. Hips or backbone protruding in bold relief are indicative of one of several underlying problems. Also ascertain that the eyes are bright and alert, have no surrounding encrustations, and are not sunken into the lizard's head. Do not mistake the cryptic behavior of arboreal lizards with lethargy; the two are entirely different.

• Ask an expert. If you are a beginning hobbyist, seek the input of a herper with more experience. Take a knowledgeable person with you when you go to pick your specimen.

• Select a lizard that displays an alert demeanor when disturbed but, if possible, not one that darts into the sides of its enclosure in panic.

Adult males of the large-headed anole,
Anolis cybotes, *are a pleasing brown color.*

• Choose immature specimens when possible. Better yet, choose captive-bred and -hatched specimens whenever they are available.

• Keep in mind that not all species react in the same way to the same stimulus. Learn what to expect and make your choice based on this knowledge. If you are a beginner, choose an easily kept, hardy species with which to begin your hobby.

• Ask if the lizard can be handled easily; some species can be handled more readily than others. For instance, young green water dragons are more easily handled and tamed than basilisks of similar size.

Handling

Lizards, in general, are not creatures that enjoy being restrained. Some individuals and species object to it more than others. Of the anoles, basilisks, and other lizard groups that we discuss in this book, it is usually only the water dragons that become tame enough to handle—and even they don't really care for it. To many lizards, being handled, being restrained, is to be subjugated—dominated. The natural instinct of any lizard is to be the dominant, not the dominated. So, your desire to handle and restrain your pet works against its every natural instinct. Some lizards will become quiescent and will submit to handling; some won't. Those that do will often make a break for freedom at any given opportunity. We strongly suggest that you handle these lizards as little as possible—that you enjoy them for their natural beauty and for the beauty of the terraria that you create for them.

If you do have to handle these lizards, be gentle but firm. When you do find it necessary to hold or restrain one of these lizards, remember that even a small specimen can and will bite, and larger types can do so painfully hard. Grip them with that in mind. With small specimens enfold neck and body in one hand. With larger specimens, enfold neck and shoulders with one hand and with the other immobilize the rear legs and give the body support.

To clip the nails of your lizard, hold the foot firmly and snip off the tip with nail clippers.

If you are bitten, don't rip your hand free and don't drop the lizard. Pulling your hand sharply free can cause a more severe laceration and can tear teeth from your lizard's mouth or otherwise injure its jaws. Dropping it can result in damage to its internal organs, broken bones, or the escape of your lizard. Although arboreal species may be a little more accustomed to an occasional fall, they still should not be handled carelessly, and, should one of these tropical lizards escape in a different climate, the death of the lizard is a certainty with the onset of cold weather. "Wild" non-native lizards are not welcome in most human neighborhoods.

Claw Clipping

Large lizards with sharp claws can be uncomfortable to handle, either casually as pets or just when necessary. Using fingernail clippers, the very tip (the tiny point that projects downward) of each claw can be removed as necessary. Do not cut into the vein that is present in each claw. Should you accidentally do so, stem the bleeding with alum or a styptic pencil.

Sources for Obtaining Your Lizards

Pet Stores

Although the more common anoles are usually readily available in pet stores across the nation and in Europe, you may need to find a specialty dealer to find the more uncommon anoles, basilisks, water and sail-tailed dragons. Such suppliers advertise in the classified sections of reptile magazines. Larger pet stores in large cities often have a more extensive reptile section than small-town shops. Dealing with a local pet store has its benefits, not the least of which is being able to actually see the animal in which you are interested. Unfortunately, support information from pet store employees may not always be reliable.

Mail Order

When you deal by mail order, it is not possible to see the animal, but specialty dealers are often well aware of the subtle and overt needs of the species in question. Most dealers do an excellent job of portraying the animals they have on hand.

The continued existence of a mail order reptile dealer is dependent on satisfied return customers. Specialty dealers benefit from earned reputations of integrity.

Breeders

Breeders, whether specialized hobbyists or commercial breeders, are one of the best sources of parasite-free, well-acclimated specimens and accurate information. Most breeders keep records of genetics, lineage, fecundity, health, and the quirks of the specimens with which they work.

With proper care, lizards can live quite normal life spans in captivity. For the smaller anole species, this seems to be in the four- to eight-year range, but for the larger anoles, basilisks, water dragons, and sail-tailed lizards, a life span can be from ten to fifteen years or, rarely, longer. Therefore, if you choose your specimen(s) carefully and offer them the proper regimen of care, the chances are quite good that you and your chosen pet lizard will spend many years together.

Remember to wash your hands before and after handling each of your lizards, for their health as well as for your own.

Develop and keep the habit of washing your hands before and after handling your lizards.

These records are invariably available to their customers. Lizard breeders can be found in the classified ads of the various reptile-oriented magazines now on the market (see Information, page 91).

Shipping Information

There is a good chance that the specimen(s) you seek will be available only from a specialty dealer or breeder who is located some distance from you. In this case, you'll need to have the specimens you wish to purchase shipped to you by mail or air freight. For a hobbyist who has not done this before, shipping may seem intimidating, but the chances are excellent that your supplier is quite familiar with shipping and will be delighted to assist you in any way possible.

FINDING YOUR OWN LIZARDS

You may choose to collect your own lizard. However, before doing so, be certain to learn all pertinent rules and regulations, including whether the lizard in which you are interested is protected. It is as important to adhere to international regulations and laws as it is to comply with those in the United States or Europe.

Many hobbyists discover that seeing and catching their lizards from the wild is more satisfying than purchasing them from their local pet emporiums. Some hobbyists merely pick up a pair or two of anoles while on a Florida vacation, but other hobbyists actually create their vacations around the probability of collecting anoles and other herps.

Lizards in the United States

Since it is to Florida and Latin America that many American and European vacationers travel, we have limited this chapter to the finding of lizards in these regions. Several anoles and at least one basilisk species—the northern brown—are now firmly established in

The Philippine sail-tailed dragon, **Hydrosaurus pustulatus,** *is now being bred by a few hobbyists.*

Florida, but neither water dragons nor sail-tailed lizards are yet known to be found there.

Northern brown basilisks, although usually associated with quiet waters, are now common in many heavily overgrown fields and road edges in Dade County, Florida. As might be expected, the lizards are especially common along the overgrown edges of canals. Where present, these admirably camouflaged lizards may be seen at the edges of clearings, atop limestone boulders, and on low limbs in shrubby growth.

Northern brown basilisks are wary, with adult males being particularly difficult to approach. The babies are easier to approach than adults of either sex, but this is merely a comparison.

Nearly impossible to catch by hand, if approached slowly and obliquely, the diurnal, heliothermic basilisk may occasionally be caught in a long-handled field net. More often they are noosed. Gentleness and removing the lizards as quickly as possible from the noose are mandatory. Brown basilisks may occasionally be found sleeping on a limb at night. If approached stealthily, they may then be caught by hand.

Green anoles should be looked for by day as they sun on the trunks of trees, telephone poles, garden fences, and similar areas. At night they may sleep on a low leaf or a blade of grass, where they are easily seen by flashlight. In the warmer portions of their range (Florida and the lower Rio Grande Valley), anoles may be found year-round.

Brown anoles are a "low to the ground" species that can be found in shrubs, on roadside signs, fences, trash piles, fallen limbs, and tree trunks—even the walls of sheds and houses.

Other anole species can be found by heading southward to Dade and Broward Counties in Florida. To be most successful, hunt during the summer months, when even canopy species descend to lower elevations in the trees.

The little gray to pea-green bark anoles, A. distichus ssp., are usually seen in thickets of low shrubbery. They are not uncommon near houses, but have expanded their ranges outward from urban areas along the canal systems. Tangles of bougainvillea, Surinam cherry, and crotons are favored habitats. Since these small lizards are difficult to keep in captivity, we always suggest merely looking at them. Take photographs rather than specimens.

For the knight anole, begin on a hot, humid summer morning and look for them low on the tree trunks. They hang, head down, and their yellow shoulder markings and huge pink dewlaps (both sexes have dewlaps) render them quite conspicuous. Knight anoles seem to favor broad-leafed exotic evergreen trees such as

Ficus and Schleffera but may occasionally be seen in poincianas, jacarandas, and Australian pines, especially in summer, when these latter trees are fully leafed.

Before you make a grab for a knight anole, remember, these lizards bite—and they bite hard! They will try to avoid capture, but if they feel threatened and do not feel escape is possible, they will jump at your hand and bite.

Although you can now find knight anoles all over Miami and surrounding towns, they seem particularly common in Coral Gables, where they may be seen on Ficus trees used in median plantings.

The Jamaican giant anole, A. garmani, is a big anole that looks superficially like a gigantic green anole. It can be found in some of the larger trees in Dade and Lee counties. The males can exceed a foot in length, and because of their newness in the wilds of urban Florida, these pretty anoles are currently more coveted than the larger knight anoles. Many homeowners take a protective attitude toward these bright green, non-agressive lizards.

Jamaican giants seem to descend lower in the trees during the hot, humid days of summer. They are often seen in large jacaranda and poinciana trees when the trees are sparsely leafed in winter. Spotting them when the trees have full foliage is just about impossible. Where they are persecuted by collectors for the pet trade, the lizards become very wary.

The Puerto Rican crested anole, A. c. cristatellus, was found several years ago in Dade County, Florida. Like the brown anole, with which it might be confused, the crested anole usually positions itself low on tree trunks, fences, or trash piles. Crested anoles are now widespread and common in southern Dade County.

Lizards in Other Countries

There are times when your vacation may take you out of the United States, or, if you are an avid and advanced herper, you may actually plan a vacation that allows you to see reptiles and amphibians in the field. Remember that your visit must legally be restricted to only seeing and perhaps photographing the animals in the wild.

Permits are needed if you plan to collect them, export them from the country of origin, or import them to the United States.

On a recent trip to the Peruvian Amazon, among the approximately 90 species of reptiles and amphibians found, we were fortunate enough to see six species of anoles. Unlike the anoles in the United States, which are often numerous, we searched long and hard for the few specimens we did find. While some were seen during the daylight hours, the sightings occurred only after extended hikes, often in driving rains. Others, among these the beautiful *A. transversalis*, were found by flashlight at night, again usually after long, muddy hikes that took us deep into the rain forests.

A. transversalis is a large, beautiful, and sexually dimorphic species. No matter what their ground color, the females we saw were prominently marked with the broad transverse bands from which their specific name is derived. Even their rather small, off-white or light yellow dewlap was transversely banded with dark spots. While the body bands of the males were discernible, they had been infiltrated with dark specks and flecks and were poorly defined. The variably colored but often yellow dewlap of adult males is immense. It extends rearward to mid-venter. Like most other anoles that assume a green coloration, *A. transversalis* is highly arboreal. The several specimens of the 10-inch-long (25 cm) anole that we saw were all found at varying heights in rain forest trees.

We found two other anole species on or near the forest floor, among the fallen leaves that camouflaged them admirably. Both were shade-dwelling brown species that attain about 7 inches (17.8 cm) in total length. These were the robust and angular *A. bombiceps* and the very similar and sympatric *A. nitens chrysolepis*. The two differ in very minimal ways, but the dewlaps of the *A. bombiceps* we found were predominantly blue, while those of the *A. n. chrysolepis* were blue-centered, red-edged, and bore numerous whitish scales in the blue field when distended.

Three smaller, brownish species were also found. Although the first of these, the pale brown *A. aurofuscata*, was not uncommon on the isolated clearing trees along the various riverbanks, the other two seemed of more terrestrial habits. Even the dewlap of *A. aurofuscatus* was pale and varied from reddish to almost yellow. Those we observed were alert and difficult to approach, darting upward from the trunk to the foliage as we neared. This is a small anole species, averaging about 5 inches (12.7 cm) in length. The single *A. ortonii* that we found was an adult female. She was clad in a pale tannish gray and bore a vague, irregular, lineate pattern on her sides and back. The average-sized dewlap of the male can vary from yellow-orange to a rather bright red, or can even be bicolored.

The final species we saw was the rather inconspicuous *A. trachyderma*. It has a variable brown dorsum and a variable (orange-yellow to orange-red) dewlap and was found low on clearing trees and fallen, forest-edge leaf litter.

CAGING

Determining the most satisfactory caging for a lizard may take some thought. The kind of cage used will vary according to the amount and type of space you have available. Where will you be keeping your lizards? Will you keep them indoors in a limited space, indoors in a more spacious area, on your outdoor patio, or elsewhere?

Outdoor Caging Suggestions

We find keeping lizards outdoors infinitely more satisfying than keeping them in small indoor terraria. Although at some latitudes keeping them outside would be only a summer option (and then only with nighttime heat from above-cage heat bulbs), when and where possible we strongly suggest outdoor mainte-nance. We try always to provide a cage large enough for a breeding colony.

Reptariums that have reinforced nylon screening over a tubular frame are now avail-able in many sizes and shapes. These stand up well to outside conditions and provide ideal habitats for anoles and immature basilisks and

Adult male brown water dragons have black ear markings, contrasting body bands, a low crest, and a red chest.

water dragons. We make 6-foot high, "step-in" cages of half-inch welded wire wrapped around a frame of 2 × 4s, fastened to a ⁵⁄₈-inch plywood bottom which is affixed to large casters. These work well for the larger species.

Although it may take some effort, the cages can be moved inside during inclement weather, or outside on pleasant days to allow the lizards natural sunlight and rain. The cage furniture consists of a suitably sized cage-height *Ficus* tree (usually *F. benjamina*) and a number of dead limb perches of suitable diameter.

Cage Sizes

While the large (step-in) cages are our prefer-ence, especially for the water dragons, basilisks, and larger anoles, we have used smaller cages equally well for both large and small species. We have successfully kept small anoles and babies of the larger lizard species in caging as small as a 20-gallon (75.7 L) terraria. Adults of the various basilisks and water dragons should be in cages no smaller than 55-gallon (208 L) show tanks. We always incorporate some type of potted plant as well as horizontal perching limbs into the decor. Smaller wood and wire cages that offer greater ventilation than converted aquaria can also be constructed. In the high humidity of Florida, we actually prefer the former.

Vertical Caging

A cage containing a pair or trio of Jamaican giant or knight anoles should measure about 4 feet long × 2.5 feet wide × 6 feet high (1.22 m × 0.76 m × 1.83 m). A cage containing more than that number should be about 6 feet × 2.5 feet × 6 feet (1.83 m × 0.76 m × 1.83 m).

Horizontal Caging

We provide vertically oriented terraria/cages for arboreal species, but for lizards that are more terrestrial we strive to offer a proportionately greater amount of horizontal space. By using $1/8$-inch (3.18 mm) mesh in the cage construction, we prevent the escape of all but the smallest food insects.

Indoor Caging Suggestions

Many enthusiasts actually begin keeping reptiles because they have neither the time, space, nor ability to keep a dog, cat, or bird. This is especially true of apartment dwellers, many of whom are faced with regulations prohibiting so-called "normal" pets. Reptiles of many kinds can, on the other hand, be kept in enclosed indoor quarters. If certain conditions are met by their keepers, lizards, too, can be satisfying, long-lived, indoor pets, but be advised that the vivaria for most lizards will need more thought

and somewhat more sophisticated equipment than would the terrarium for a snake.

Anoles, basilisks, and water dragons are among the types of lizards that are often first chosen by hobbyists. All can and will thrive indoors. Since most anoles are small and highly arboreal, they can be kept in proportionately tall terraria of rather small lateral dimensions. The larger size and more active horizontal lifestyle of basilisks and water dragons dictate that these creatures be provided with proportionately more terrarium floor space. Adequate height is also important.

In the wild, the arboreal anole species currently available in the American pet trade may alter their preferred microhabitats by season (and/or ambient temperature). For example, the impressive knight anole, *A. equestris*, may remain high in the canopy, where thermoregulation is relatively easy during the cooler months of the year. When ambient temperatures warm to or above its preferred minimum (thus making thermoregulation largely unnecessary), the big lizard descends the trunks to just a few feet above the ground. We have noticed the same tendency with the Jamaican giant anole, *A. garmani*, but rather than remaining in the dense canopy, during the winter this species tends to bask high on the trunks and upper branches of seasonally sparsely leaved trees (such as poinciana and jacaranda). Jamaican giant anoles also descend to about head level on tree trunks during the warmer months. Captive anoles seem to fare best in vertically oriented cages.

Humidity

Excessive humidity may be a concern in some regions or during some seasons and may become a paramount concern when living plants are used in terraria. Using a commercial screen top will help. If the tank becomes too dry, adding a piece of Plexiglas to the screen top will help hold moisture inside the tanks.

Vertically Oriented Tanks

Large aquaria (55- to 100-gallon, or 189–378.5 L) may be oriented vertically. When positioned in this manner, the top (which has now become a side) must be covered. To facilitate the usage of a commercial top, you will need to keep the frame of the tank at least one-half inch (12.7 mm) above the surface on which it sits. This can be accomplished by placing a number of rubber stoppers, which can be purchased in hardware stores, between the stand and the tank.

Commercial tops can be clipped into place, but when they are used, the whole side opens at once for access. While such a large opening certainly provides easy access for cleaning, it also allows nervous lizards an easy avenue of escape. It is much safer to have the access to the open side divided into two, or even three, separate entry panels with at least one—the bottom—being glass. The glass panel can be held firmly and tightly in place by a continuous bead of aquarium sealant on the two sides and the bottom. A screen top can be clipped into

place on top of the glass panel; just make sure that you've smoothed and taped the open edge of the glass so you don't cut yourself when you reach into the tank.

Horizontally Oriented Tanks for Basilisks and Water Dragons

Some of these lizards will do well in terraria oriented in precisely the way the lizards were designed to be oriented—horizontally. Those

The horizontal format wood and wire cage provides an active lizard such as a basilisk room to roam, but make sure there are enough visual barriers to make the lizard feel secure.

This pair of green basilisks has a large cage, limbs for climbing and basking, and a pool for swimming.

lizards are the four species of basilisks and two species of water dragons.

Because of their active lifestyles, basilisks and water dragons should be given the largest possible cages. We suggest a minimum size of 100 gallons (378.5 L)—and preferably twice that—for a pair of adult specimens.

Visual barriers. Many basilisks, and to a somewhat lesser degree, water dragons, are nervous and quick to be frightened. This is especially true of wild-collected specimens. These lizards, unused to transparent restraints (such as glass) in the wild, may continually batter their noses in their efforts to escape. A profusion of visual barriers in their cages, such as horizontal and diagonal limbs and vining vegetation (either real or artificial), may help these

A young male northern brown basilisk.

Brown on green? The color of the green anole has little to do with the color of the surface on which it is resting.

lizards feel more secure. You should always move slowly when you are near the vivarium.

Even with visual barriers and slow movement, we have, in many cases, found it necessary to tape sheets of paper or plasticized backings over most of the glass surfaces of the cage. These opaque barriers not only provide the lizards with additional security, they help the lizards know when they are near the edges of their vivarium.

Always provide enough visual barriers to make the lizard feel secure. Separate sun- (or lamp-) warmed, horizontal limbs and perches should be provided for all specimens, or only the dominant lizard will use a perch.

Cage Furniture and Accessories for Horizontally Oriented Tanks

"Naturalistic" caging. One of the things we like best about keeping these interesting lizards is that they do better in brightly lit, beautifully planted, botanically interesting facilities than in the starkness so often associated with the cages used by American herpetoculturists. Vining plants, bromeliads, small orchids, or other plant species that thrive in high humidity situations can be used singly or in combination, and lichened limbs, mosses, and attractively shaped colored and arranged rocks are all sought by vivarists.

Plants. Among the vining plants, several of the philodendrons and pothos are excellent choices. All thrive under reduced light and in high-humidity situations. Non-vining (also called "self-heading") forms of philodendrons and anthuriums also do well. Small species of bromeliads (air plants) can be positioned either in the soil or wired onto limbs, where, if misted occasionally and given sufficient light, they will thrive and spread. Small epiphytic orchids can accompany the bromeliads on elevated boughs, and if conditions are suitable, some of the

Use a variety of plants and wood pieces to add visual barriers to your cage.

hardiest forms will multiply and bloom. Old limbs, most festooned with arboreal ferns and/or lichens, are strewn on our woodland floor. We utilize some of the prettier ones in our terraria.

Rocks and perches. Pitted (oolitic) limestone rocks and boulders are found all over Florida, and other kinds of rock formations, some mossy, some lichenate, some simply pretty in their stratifications, can be gathered in other parts of the world. Hobbyists can find rocks, manzanita, cholla (cactus) skeletons, and other decorations in pet stores. Rocky formations seem less desirable for these lizards than limbs, but may certainly be incorporated into the overall vivarium setups. We caution you to be sure that, when rocks are used, they are placed firmly and cannot shift position—even if your lizards should try to burrow beneath them.

Positioning perches. Anoles like their perches high up in their terraria, and most will preferen-

tially choose to bask on a horizontal or diagonal perch rather than a vertical (or nearly vertical) one. Smaller species also readily use leaves and grasses as perching and sleeping stations. Horizontal or diagonal perches can be held in place wherever you want them in the terrarium by simply placing a suitably wide and deep U-shaped bead of aquarium sealant (open side up) on the glass ends of the tank and, once the sealant has dried, dropping the limb into place.

Although adept climbers, basilisks and water dragons preferentially bask at levels lower than those chosen by most anoles.

Large anole species will occasionally climb on yielding twig tips, but they, along with the basilisks and water dragons, prefer perches of at least the diameter of their bodies. In community (multi-lizard) setups, several equally prominent perches are better than a single one. This is especially true when the community setups involve more than a single species, each with its single dominant male.

Substrate. The substrate of your terrarium may be as varied as the furniture. Although it is not particularly aesthetic (especially in an otherwise "naturalistic" setup), layers of newspaper or paper towels can be used on the bottom. These have the advantage of being absorbent, inexpensive, readily available, and easily changed. Should you choose, a layer of fallen leaves can be gathered up and spread over the paper. We usually use only a thick layer of fallen leaves. Because they are durable and easy to work with, we use the leaves of live oaks, *Quercus virginiana*, in our terraria, replacing them with new when necessary.

Hide boxes. Basilisks (occasionally) and water dragons (frequently) will use hiding areas if they are provided. Easily cleaned and sterilized plastic caves—some incorporating water dishes in their designs—are stocked by many pet shops.

Anoles prefer elevated hiding areas. A hollowed or slotted limb or a piece of hollowed cholla cactus skeleton suspended near the top of the terrarium will usually be used extensively by these treetop sprites.

Such items as "hot rocks" and "heat limbs" are available, but we do not encourage their use (see comments in heating and lighting sections, pages 29–31).

Cagemates

Although the anoles, basilisks, and water dragons are not as solitary as some lizards, the males are still highly territorial. It is usually impossible—and never particularly desirable—to keep more than a single sexually mature male of a given species, or of a closely allied species, in each cage. Intraspecific aggression among males can be persistent and fatal. If not crowded, you may usually keep from one to several adult females with each male. Although the females are usually somewhat less aggressive toward each other, hierarchies may be formed. You must ascertain that all subordinate specimens continue to feed and drink adequately, are allowed to bask, and are not unduly stressed by the dominant female. Juveniles of both sexes can be housed together, although growth may be more rapid if only a single specimen is kept per container.

Given a large enough cage, it may be possible to keep two diverse species of anoles, such as a green and a brown, or another combination of these lizards, together. For instance, we have successfully kept knight anoles and green basilisks together, and have seen brown basilisks

Water dragons like to bask on sturdy limbs above water.

kept with green water dragons. In neither combination did the two species show the slightest interest in each other. Other combinations are equally possible. Experiment, but watch closely for adverse reactions. We have successfully kept compatibly sized day geckos, White's and other large tree frogs, and a fair number of other nonaggressive lizard species caged with anoles, basilisks, and water dragons.

Thermoregulation

Every reptile has a body temperature at which all daily functions are optimized; lizards are no exception to this rule. Like other reptiles, lizards attain this preferred temperature by thermoregulation. Thermoregulation—the altering of body temperature by external means—can mean either warming or cooling, as necessary, and can be accomplished in various ways. Certain lizards, especially nocturnal and/or high-altitude forms, may lay on top of or beneath sun-warmed rocks

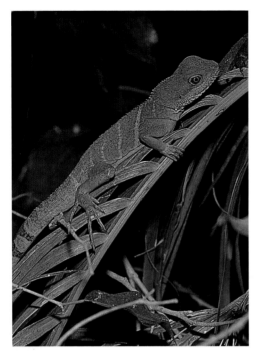

A baby green water dragon perches comfortably on the midrib of a palm frond.

Warm from Above

Because they are heliotherms, we recommend that the anoles, basilisks, and water dragons be warmed, as well as illuminated naturally, from above. We strongly feel that warmth-producing flood- and spotlights directed onto/into basking areas (either preferred areas of the terrarium floor or a limb near the cage top) are much more satisfactory for thermoregulation than are the electrified artificial limbs and rocks now available.

Bulb Wattage

Vary the wattage of the bulb(s) according to terrarium size. Basking temperatures for most of these lizards can be maintained in a 20-gallon (75.6 L) terrarium by a 50-watt plant floodlight, especially if it is directed toward a tank-top limb. Heating an area on the terrarium floor might require the more directed rays of a spotlight bulb. Attaining the same suitable temperatures in a stacked 100-gallon (378.5 L) terrarium may require a 150- or 200-watt bulb. Suitably heating the terrarium will require smaller bulbs in warm conditions than in cooler ones.

or logs. To cool themselves, they merely move away from the warmed object against which they have been lying. Lizards that thermoregulate in this manner are termed thigmothermic. However, most lizards, at least most with which hobbyists are familiar, are heliothermic, which means that to warm themselves, these lizards seek sun-warmed/sunlit areas in which to bask. They are physiologically adapted to being warmed primarily from above. Although the little casque-headed lizards of the genus *Corytophanes* seem to indulge in heliothermic behavior less than most others, most anoles and relatives, basilisks and relatives, and water dragons are heliotherms.

Caution

The directed rays of even a rather small bulb can easily melt the plastic now used on aquarium frames. The heat from large bulbs can even break aquarium glass. Too large a bulb can overheat your terrarium, and the high temperatures can be lethal to your lizards. Also, rays from misdirected or oversized bulbs can burn and kill plant leaves. When using lights or heaters of any kind, always use extreme care!

Temperatures

Anoles, basilisks, and water dragons like warm temperatures and high relative humidity. Although species from the forest floor may be adapted to cooler temperatures (but higher humidity) than the forest-edge and savanna species, the variance is by only a very few degrees. Species from high altitudes (of which there are currently few in the pet trade) may be adapted to colder nighttime lows than lowland species, but would still thermoregulate extensively during their daytime hours of activity.

Suggestions for preferred habitat and temperature range are provided in the species account section of this book. If you are not sure what temperature your species prefers, we suggest erring slightly on the side of warmth.

Day Versus Night

A cage that is maintained in the high 80s°F (27°C–32°C) by day and in the low 70s°F (21°C–23°C) or high 60s°F (19°C–21°C) by night will prove ideal for most anoles and for all basilisks and water dragons. Except for forest floor species, a high level of full-spectrum illumination is desirable. Provide a warmed basking area (surface temperature of about 95°F, or 38.8°C) during the hours of daylight by prudent use of a floodlight. Many anoles preferentially bask while positioned head downward on a tree trunk. Other anoles and the basilisks and water dragons may bask on a horizontal limb, on top of thick vegetation, or on the ground.

Accommodate all possibilities by providing suitably sized limbs positioned both vertically and horizontally.

The actual heating may be accomplished in several ways.

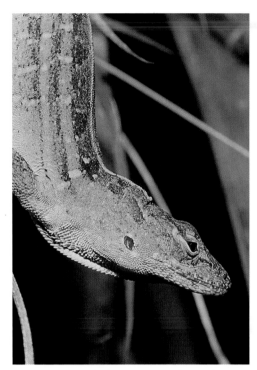

Head down and alert—a typical pose for the brown anole.

Area warming. The method that we most favor for area warming is the prudent use of directed bulbs (flood or spot). Undertank heaters, placed under a portion of a cage, can be used in conjunction with directed overhead lighting.

Caution

Glass terraria will not only filter out most of the beneficial UV-A and UV-B rays, but even on a cool day glass will concentrate the rays of the sun, causing your terrarium to quickly, and lethally, overheat.

The wood and wire cage on casters is easy to move.

Such heaters, made specifically for this purpose, are available in most pet shops. Human heating pads may also be adapted as undertank heaters. Be advised that the use of an undertank heater beneath the water receptacle may overheat the water (and the lizards will refuse to drink it) and will assuredly increase cage humidity.

A few degrees of warmth and additional humidity can be gained by placing an aquarium heater in a tall, slim jar of water and taping the jar in place in a not easily seen corner of the tank. If you do use this method, be sure that your lizards cannot purposely or accidentally enter the jar and drown or jostle and break the heater. Add only warm-to-hot water to replace the evaporated water, or the temperature change will break the heater sheath.

Hibernation

Of all of the species mentioned in these pages, hibernation, a period of winter dormancy (also called brumation), could be considered for only two: North American green anoles, *Anolis carolinensis*, from the northernmost populations, and the southern-temperate Australian (or brown) water dragon, *Physignathus lesueurii*, from the southernmost populations. Since it is difficult, or impossible, to ascertain the origin of any given specimen once it has entered the pet trade, it is probably best to not consider hibernation for pet specimens of either. If you wish to breed your water dragons, use extreme caution (see HOW-TO: Hibernating the Brown Water Dragon, pages 66–67).

Lighting

Outside Caging

If you are using outside cages of wood and wire construction, properly lighting and heating them will be a simple matter during the late spring, summer, and early fall months in most temperate climes. For those of us in southern Florida or the lower Rio Grande valley in Texas, it should be relatively easy year-round. Simply wheel or carry your cages to a sunny spot outdoors and let nature take its course. Natural, unfiltered sunlight is the best of all possible lighting, providing the normal, beneficial amounts of UV-A and UV-B, and warmth for the animal.

Inside Caging

Proper lighting is very important to the well-being of your lizards. Heliothermic (sun-basking) lizards require proper illumination to induce activity. This is true even when conditions are otherwise optimum. Forest species may require slightly less light than those from more open settings.

Indoor caging facilities should be provided with both a heat-producing flood lamp (we use plant-grow bulbs for this function, but full-spectrum [actually color-corrected] incandescents are now available) as well as full-spectrum fluorescent lighting. The latter provides your specimens with at least some UV-A and UV-B. Although the necessity of ultraviolet rays in reptile husbandry still requires additional research, the full-spectrum fluorescent bulbs do seem to induce a rather normal activity pattern, and just may assist reptiles in synthesizing vitamin D_3, or at least in metabolizing calcium. Certainly, you should do everything possible to provide your captive lizards with the conditions that best promote the most normal life and lifestyle.

Greenhouses

Bigger Is Better

As hobbyists progress from novice to advanced status, many decide that they truly enjoy the hobby of reptile keeping and expand the scope of their hobbies in many ways. Some expand collections and some may specialize but delve more deeply into the natural history or the reproductive biology of the species in which they have developed the most interest. Often, both schools decide that they would like bigger and better facilities.

What could be bigger and better than a reptile-dedicated greenhouse? While it is certainly true that greenhouses are a luxury item, they are more in vogue today than ever before. And, like other caging facilities, they can be purchased in either a kit or prebuilt product, or they can be homemade. They can be simply elaborate, or elaborately simple. In many areas, greenhouses are considered permanent structures, and a building permit is required to legally install one.

Anoles, basilisks, water and sail-tailed dragons, and their allies are ideal greenhouse lizards. They all thrive in highly humid, lushly planted situations. They may be either kept caged inside the greenhouse, or let loose to roam the entire structure. We favor the latter concept. However, all lizards are far more adept at escaping their caging facilities than even the most agile of plants, and the glass-climbing anoles are especially so. The lizard greenhouse must be secure in every aspect, and should have double-entry doors as an enhanced containment system. Windows and ventilators, either low or along the ridgepole, must be tightly screened from the inside. Heating and cooling units must be entirely screened to prevent injury to the lizards.

Building a Greenhouse

Building a greenhouse is fun. While securing it as a lizard house can be tedious, the end result will provide you with years of satisfaction.

Landscaping

Rock formations and waterfalls may be bedecked with mosses, ferns, selaginellas, and

When landscaped with imagination, the interior of even a small greenhouse can be your own bit of rain forest habitat and, as such, can provide a healthy and secure habitat for your lizards that could not be otherwise attained.

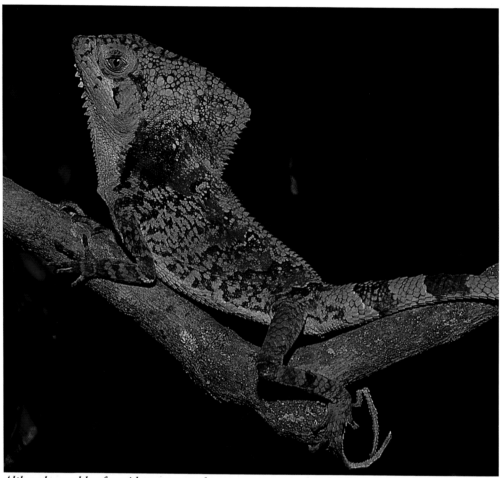

Although capable of rapid movement, the common casque-headed lizard, Corytophanes cristata, *depends on camouflage to avoid detection.*

episcias, small sunken ponds may be replete with blooming tropical water lilies, while lush growths of philodendrons, epipremnums, and syngoniums create secure tangles. Weathered tree skeletons may be used for perches—only your imagination and your pocketbook will limit the possibilities.

Construction tips. We suggest that the base be sunk a foot (0.3 m) or more below the surface of the ground and that whenever possible, insulating, double glazing be used. We learned that the higher cost of the latter is quickly offset by the ease (and savings) with which the finished structure may be heated or cooled.

Cuban bearded anoles vary in color between gray and deep brown.

Although neither of us is a gifted carpenter, we do enjoy building our own cages.

Our outside cages reside in sunlit splendor on a wooden deck. We build all of our cages as large as feasibly possible, since we intend them to be used year-round. We also proportion them so that they can be rolled inside. If the cage you are intending to build will be used only during the warmth of summer (taking the lizards indoors during cool/cold weather), movability and dimensions will be less critical.

With that in mind, we suggest that you first determine how much space you have. Besides determining how big the finished cage will be, the available space should help you decide what kind (or at least what size range) of lizards you'll be keeping. The following instructions and material list enable you to build a cage (with rounded corners) approximately 32 inches wide, 48 inches long, and 72 inches high (81.3 cm × 122 cm × 183 cm) (plus caster height). By not rounding the corners of the bottom and top, you can cut down considerably on your work as well as reduce by four the number of 2 × 2s needed.

Materials

The materials you will need are as follows:

Marine plywood, 1 × 2s, 2 × 2s, and wire mesh are used in making your own movable cage.

- Two pieces of ¾-inch (19.1 mm) thick marine plywood, 32 inches × 48 inches (81 cm × 122 cm) Marine plywood, 1 × 2s, 2 × 2s, and wire mesh are used in making your own movable cage.
- Straight 2 × 2s (we use treated lumber and have never had any problems). You'll need at least 13 eight-footers (2.4 m)
- Thin wooden or galvanized facing strips to face the inside of the door opening
- ⅛-inch (3.18 mm) mesh welded wire hardware cloth. We buy ours by the roll in 36 inch (91 cm) heights. You will need about 30 feet (9.1 m) per cage.
- Galvanized nails
- A few feet of thin, pliable, single-strand wire
- Staples
- Two sturdy hinges and two hooks and eyes
- Saw, hammer, staple gun, tape measure or yardstick, and screwdriver

Since our building methods are not precise, we precut only the 10 upright braces to 5 feet 10 inches (177.8 cm) in length and the plywood top and bottom. Horizontal braces and door are measured and cut to exact length or size as we build.

OUTDOOR CAGE

Top and Bottom of the Cage

We first tackle the top and the bottom of the cage. Because of the constant high humidity and frequent rains in Florida, we use marine plywood of 3/4-inch (19.1 mm) thickness for both top and bottom. The dimensions we have settled on for most cages are 32 inches × 48 inches (81.3 cm × 122 cm). We round the corners (this is optional), using an arc on an 8-inch (20 cm) diameter. Exactly the same arc must be used to round the corners of both bottom and top (we use a salad plate). Once the corners are rounded (optional), the bottom is done; however, we cut a sizable panel out of the center of the top (we usually leave a 6 inch [15.2 cm] rim on all sides and remove the rest). The hole left by the removed panel is, of course, screened.

We build the cage while it is lying on its back, first nailing the inner two uprights in place. Once those are secure, we roll the cage onto a side and nail the next two, and so on. Note that the front door has four uprights, the door hanging between the innermost two.

We build and screen the door before hanging it. We have found that a width of 2 feet (0.6) and a height of 4 feet (1.2 m) is adequate for the door. The frame is made from 2 × 2s.

Place the cage on its back to staple the wire mesh in place.

Finishing the Cage

Because the 1/8-inch (3.18 m) hardware cloth we use is in 3 foot (0.9 m) heights, and we run it horizontally, horizontal cross braces are necessary between the main uprights. These are positioned about 2 feet 11 inches (88.9 cm) below the top (or above the bottom) of the cage.

The wire is overlapped slightly and stapled along both its top and bottom edges. The overlapping wire is then laced together with pliable single-strand wire along all of the corner arcs. Be sure the hardware cloth is pulled tightly when it is applied and that "puckers," if any, are folded tightly and secured.

FEEDING AND WATERING YOUR LIZARDS

Anoles, basilisks, water dragons, and their relatives are primarily insectivores, but larger specimens of some larger species will also eat small mice, fruit/honey mixtures, blossoms, and some other plant materials. Captives can be acclimated to feed on insects or rodents that are easily available to us.

Getting Started

Getting the lizard to feed for the first time may not be easy. A lizard deprived of food for a lengthy period by a collector or wholesaler may need considerable prodding to begin feeding again. This is especially true of cone-headed and casque-headed lizards, which dehydrate and stress easily and quickly. Offering a variety of foods in secure and calming surroundings will, with luck, tempt your lizard into feeding. Once it has begun feeding again, it is likely that it will continue to do so, and it may even expand its horizons to a food type quite different from the one that is natural to it.

*This is an alert brown anole, **Anolis sagrei**.*

Insects

Nothing is ever quite so easy as it initially seems! So your lizards eat insects—what could be easier to provide? But, you will quickly learn that there's more to feeding insects to your lizards than just tossing a few odd crickets into the cage. You have to feed your insects well before you offer them to your amphibians. Caring properly for your feed insects is an important aspect of successful herpetological husbandry. A poorly fed or otherwise unhealthy insect offers little but bulk when fed to a reptile; therefore, offering food insects in top-notch health should be a main concern of any herpetoculturist.

The term "gut-loading" as in "G-L crickets" is used to indicate insects that are fed highly nutritious foods immediately before being

Anoles, basilisks, and water and sail-tailed dragons in captivity feed upon crickets, meal worms (both types), house flies, and wax worms.

offered as food. Calcium, vitamin D_3, fresh fruit and vegetables, fresh alfalfa and/or bean sprouts, honey and vitamin/mineral-enhanced (chick) laying mash are only a few of the foods that may be considered for gut-loading insects. A commercially prepared gut-loading diet is now available. Insects quickly lose much of their food value if not continually fed an abundance of highly nourishing food. Most insects eat continually, so it is much to the benefit of your lizards if you supply the insects with the highest possible quality diet.

In addition, immediately before they are fed to the lizards, food insects may be placed in a jar or bag with a little calcium-D_3 additive and shaken. Known familiarly as the "shake and bake method," the finely ground powder will adhere to the insects.

Except for field plankton, all feed insects, even houseflies, are commercially available. It may be your preference to avail yourself

regularly of the various commercial sources. Certainly this is less time consuming than breeding your own insects; however, by breeding your own, you can assure that the highest possible diet is continually fed to the insects. Even if you procure the insects commercially, you should begin feeding them the best diet possible.

Field Plankton

Insects straight from the wild—commonly called field plankton—have been able to choose their diet and their nutritional value reflects this. To gather them, go to an insecticide-free yard or field and sweep a suitably meshed field net back and forth through tall grasses or low shrubs. These insects, which have fed on natural native foods, are probably at their pinnacle of health. Fed immediately after collecting, the health and full guts of the insects will greatly benefit your lizards.

Crickets

The gray cricket (*Acheta domesticus*) is readily available from fishing or pet stores. Other cricket species may be hand-collected (if your patience holds out) in small numbers beneath debris in fields, meadows, and open woodlands. All species are ideal lizard fare.

Where to get them. If you use more than 500 crickets a week, purchase them directly from wholesale producers that advertise in fishing or reptile magazines. You will find the prices are quite reasonable when crickets are purchased in multiples of 1,000.

Cricket care. Crickets fed on potatoes are fine for fishing, but you need to offer them a better diet if they are to benefit your lizards. Feed your crickets a good and varied diet of your own making, or one of the nutritious, specifically formulated cricket foods now on the market. Among other foods, fresh carrots, potatoes, broccoli, oranges, squash, sprouts, and chick laying mash will be readily consumed. All foods offered to your crickets should be sprinkled with calcium/D_3, not so much for the benefit of the insects as for the benefit of the lizards to which the crickets are fed.

While crickets can get much of the moisture requirements from their fruit and vegetables, they will also appreciate a water source. Crickets will drown easily if they are given only a plain, shallow dish of water. Instead, place cotton balls, a sponge, or even pebbles or aquarium gravel in the water dish to give the crickets sufficient purchase to climb back out when they fall in (and they will).

Cricket housing. Keep crumpled newspapers, the center tubes from rolls of paper towels, or other such hiding areas in the crickets' cage. We prefer the paper towel tubes as they can be lifted and the requisite number of crickets shaken from inside them into the cage or a transportation jar. This makes handling the fast-moving, agile insects easy.

A tightly covered 20-gallon (75.7 L) long tank will temporarily house 1,000 crickets. A substrate of sawdust, soil, vermiculite, or other such medium should be present. This must be changed often to prevent the buildup of moisture (hard on the crickets) and odor from the insects (hard on you).

Grasshoppers/Locusts

Grasshoppers and locusts (*Locusta* spp. and *Shistocerca* spp. in part) are widely used as reptile and amphibian foods in European and Asian countries, and are commercially available there. In the United States, you'll have to breed them or collect them in the field. A field net will help you gather these fast-moving insects.

Do not feed lubber grasshoppers, those brightly colored, fat grasshoppers found in the southern states; the nymphs can be fatal if eaten by your specimens. The tan and buff adults seem to be less toxic, but their use as a food item is chancy.

Waxworms

The waxworm (*Galleria* spp.) is really a caterpillar, the larval stage of the wax moth found in neglected beehives. They are frequently used as fish bait and are available from bait stores. Some pet shops sell waxworms. If you need large quantities, check the ads in any reptile and amphibian magazine for wholesale distributors.

Waxworm tips. If you buy quantities of waxworms, you will need to feed them. Chick laying mash, wheat germ, honey, and yeast mixed into a syrupy paste will serve adequately as the diet for these insects; keep the unused portion in your refrigerator.

Giant Mealworms

Giant mealworms, *Zoophobas* spp., the larvae of a South American beetle, have proven to be a great food source for many insectivorous herps. They may be fed a diet of moistened chicken starting mash; bran, leafy vegetables, and apples.

Mealworms

A common food item favored by neophyte reptile and amphibian keepers, mealworms (*Tenebrio molitor*) should actually be fed sparingly, due to the large amounts of chitin they contain. They are easily kept at normal room

Northern brown basilisks have crests only on their head.

The South American sharp-nosed bush anole, **Polychrus acutirostris,** *is occasionally available in the pet trade.*

Juvenile Australian brown water dragons are hardy and now are rather readily available.

Baby green water dragons have big heads, thin necks, and a paler coloration.

temperatures in plastic receptacles containing a 2- to 3-inch (5.1–7.6 cm) layer of bran for food and a potato or apple for their moisture requirements.

Roaches

Roaches of many species are now commercially available. Consult your supplier for husbandry methods.

Houseflies

Although these may be collected as needed (weather permitting) in commercial flytraps or bred, genetically engineered flightless houseflies have recently become available. Flies and their larvae (maggots) are relished by many anoles, by cone-headed lizards, and by babies of many other forms discussed in this book.

The simplest method of introducing the adult flies to the cage is to place the entire jar inside the cage before opening it. By using this method, fewer will escape. The maggots can be removed by hand or with forceps and placed in a shallow dish.

Mice

Mice, both alive and frozen and of all sizes, are readily available. Mice can be fed in small numbers to basilisks, water dragons, and sail-tailed lizards. Some of the very large anole species, such as the Jamaican giant and the knight anoles, may also accept an occasional pinky.

Caution

DO NOT use cedar bedding for your mice; the phenols contained in cedar can be harmful to both reptiles and amphibians.

We suggest that you use aspen or pine shavings for the bedding for the mice. Feed your mice either a "lab chow" diet that is specifically formulated for them, or a healthy mixture of seeds and vegetables. Fresh water must be present at all times.

Watering

Ascertaining that your anoles, or other persistently arboreal lizard species, drink enough water may be even more difficult than monitoring their food intake. The basilisks and water dragons should pose no problems in this respect. In the wild, anoles drink pendulous droplets that either fall or condense on leaves, twigs, or even their own bodies. Simply put, anoles often (but not always) have difficulty recognizing quietly standing water as a drinking source.

When outdoors. Our step-in cages are gently sprinkled twice daily for a period of several minutes. Thirsty lizards drink copiously at these times.

Occasionally we use a second, almost as effective method of watering the lizards in these large cages. Several pinhead-sized holes are placed in the bottom of a large plastic bucket. The bucket is then filled with tap water and placed atop the cage above the ficus or above an empty water dish. The water drips slowly from the pinholes, providing the lizards with a drinking source for a quarter hour or so. Within moments after the drip system is operational, anoles and cone-headed lizards gather to drink in the uppermost foliage and, in cages with larger basilisks, the lizards station themselves in a splash zone on a sturdy inner limb or on the cage floor. The shade-loving casque-

Honey–Fruit Mix

Anoles, and to a lesser degree, basilisks and dragons, will also lap at a honey-fruit mixture. Below is the formula we use:

$^1/_3$ jar of mixed fruit or apricot strained baby food
$^1/_3$ jar of strained papaya baby food
1 teaspoon honey
$^1/_3$ eyedropper of Avitron liquid bird vitamins
$^1/_2$ teaspoon of Osteoform powdered vitamins
Add water to attain desired consistency

A small quantity of bee pollen can be added if it is available. Store any unused portion in your refrigerator, and use it within a week.

headed lizards drink the water as it trickles through the lower foliage and along the trunks and limbs.

Cages of wood and wire construction lend themselves well to these outside watering techniques. Once hitting the floor of the cage, the water merely runs out and away. The immediate runoff prevents the formation of standing water that would be detrimental to the health of your lizard. The bucket method, using a smaller bucket, can also be used in indoor terraria. Since most indoor terraria have watertight bottoms

and sides, the water accumulated in the water receptacle will need to be removed daily.

A third method can be easily adapted to either indoor or outdoor terraria/cages. As mentioned, neither anoles nor most other arboreal reptiles readily recognize quietly standing water as a drinking source. However, if that same water is roiled, as with a bubbling aquarium airstone, it is often readily recognizable. This is especially true if the water receptacles are elevated away from the bottom of the lizard's cage.

For swimmers. Water dragons and basilisks enjoy large water receptacles into which they may drop, sit, or submerge. All six of the species in these two genera are often associated with water-edge habitats in the wild. Large water/swimming containers are thus extensively used by these lizards.

"Naturalistic ponds" can be built, but even when filtered, they are usually difficult to keep clean. As unaesthetic as they may be, plastic kitty-litter pans or dish-washing tubs are among the most functional, inexpensive, and readily available water containers for larger lizards. Tubs of neutral colors do not contrast as sharply and adversely with their surroundings as those hued in bright blues, yellows, or reds. Should you choose to do so, a framework of rocks or horizontal limbs may be built to at least partially hide the outline of these containers.

YOUR LIZARDS' HEALTH

Once you have selected a healthy-looking lizard as your pet, brought it home, placed it in your caging setup, and watched it feed and drink readily, do not think the battle is over. You need to watch over your pet and observe its behavior for clues to possible illness. Your lizard deserves good treatment when it is ill.

Hydration Chambers

The uses and benefits of "hydration chambers" have long been appreciated by zoos and other public institutions. They are only now coming into general use by private herpeto-culturists and hobbyists. The term "hydration chamber" is merely a fancy term for "rain chamber." These receptacles can make the difference between life and death for dehydrated lizards, and can be used, at least partially, to replicate rainy seasons as well. As we have discussed, the seasonal rains often play an important function in the reproductive cycling of many lizards. A week or so of daily mistings in a hydration chamber will often have the same stimulating effect as natural rains.

An adult male Weber's sail-tailed dragon, **Hydrosaurus weberi,** *is an impressive lizard.*

Making your own. A hydration chamber can be constructed of wire mesh over a wood frame, or from an aquarium equipped with a circulating water pump and a screen or perforated plexiglass top. If you are fortunate enough to live in a benign climate where the cage can be placed outdoors, a mist nozzle can be placed on the end of a hose, affixed over the cage, and fresh water run through this for an hour or more a day. Neither chlorinates nor chloramines will unduly affect your lizards.

If indoors, the cage can be placed on top, or inside of, a properly drained utility tub and the fresh water system used. It is imperative that the drain system be adequate and kept free of debris if this system is used indoors. A secondary (backup) drain (just in case. . .) might do much to guarantee your peace of mind.

In contained systems, the circulation pump can force water from the tank itself through a

Use the hydration chamber to re-hydrate a newly acquired lizard.

small diameter PVC pipe into which a series of lateral holes have been drilled, or merely brought up to the top of the tank and allowed to drip through the screen or perforated plexiglass. A wire mesh false bottom serves as a resting spot for the lizard while it is in the chamber. An aquarium heater will keep the water temperature at 82–84°F.

Why use a chamber? The use of these (or similar) units can do much to help moisture-starved herptiles recuperate. Those that will most benefit from such a structure are the rain forest species that are freighted long distances to reach the pet markets of America, Asia, Europe, and other countries. Newly received anoles, casque- and cone-headed lizards, as well as baby basilisks, water dragons, and sail-tailed lizards are all prime candidates for hydration chamber treatment.

It is imperative that the water in self-contained systems be kept immaculately clean.

The Veterinarian

Making a decision of whether a $5 green or brown anole should be taken to a veterinarian when it is ailing is always difficult. Adding to the indecision is the sad fact that, once a lizard as small as an anole begins to look sick, it is often too ill to save, no matter how heroic the veterinary intervention. Perhaps because they are larger and more costly, lizard keepers seem to have less problem seeking medical help for basilisks, water dragons, and sail-tailed dragons when necessary.

Many of us ask whether we shouldn't just "let nature take her course" and then replace the lizard if it dies. That is really a personal decision, but we feel that any pet lizard is deserving of whatever help we are able to offer. Once the lizard has been removed from the wild, we, not Mother Nature, are in charge of its well-being—its destiny. And, even if you are unable to save that particular lizard, after seeing it your veterinarian may be able to offer suggestions that will prevent a replay of the scenario with your next lizard.

Finding a qualified reptile veterinarian is not always an easy task. The veterinary care of reptiles and amphibians is a specialized discipline. An association of reptile veterinarians provides regular interchanges of ideas, technology, and accepted practices among the member specialists. Veterinarians do not necessarily have to be members to be competent in the care of reptiles and amphibians, but this professional association does help them remain abreast of new technology.

Find a Veterinarian Early

By the time anoles, basilisks, and water dragons (or any other lizards, for that matter) manifest external signs of ailments, they are usually very ill. Therefore, we strongly suggest that you locate a reptile veterinarian before you need one and discuss the costs of office visits and medications in advance. It neither costs less nor takes less time for a veterinarian to look at and treat an anole than it does to perform the same service on a cat or dog. As a matter of fact, because of the small size of the anole and the toxicity of some medications to reptiles, treating the anole will necessarily be more exacting.

Nutrition-related Maladies

Metabolic Bone Disease (MBD)

Symptoms. MBD is typified by the softening of the bones. Pliability in the lower jawbones, kinking of the tail, limb swelling, and lack of rigidity in the leg bones are all diagnostic signs.

This is perhaps the most common insidious and pervasive disease that you (and your lizard) are apt to encounter. Yet it is completely preventable! MBD is known by several other names as well, among them decalcification, demineralization, and fibrous osteodystrophy. Improper metabolization of calcium, or insufficient quantities of calcium available, causes this disease.

Since this is a disease encountered time and again, let's take a more extensive look at the problem, and discuss how to avoid it.

Problem areas. Watching and correcting five potential problem areas will help you stave off MBD:

1. Provide unfiltered natural sunlight (best) or full-spectrum lighting (distant second).

2. Provide vitamin D_3.

3. Provide calcium.

4. The dietary calcium:phosphorus ratio must be a minimum of 2:1 (3:1 is even better).

5. Do not feed omnivorous lizards plant materials containing oxalic acid (a calcium binder; among others, spinach and oxalis, or wood sorrel, are such plants).

Here are the reasons for the above five points:

Ultraviolet rays (UV-B), from natural sunlight, or from artificial sources, help reptiles synthesize vitamin D_3 in the skin. Without the presence of D_3, calcium, even when amply provided, cannot be properly metabolized. Sadly, the vast majority of most bulbs now on the market do not provide a great deal of UV. This includes many that are currently billed as full-spectrum. No, or reduced, UV-B equals no, or reduced, D_3 synthesis; thus, an artificial source of D_3 must be provided. Vitamin D_3 must be present for the reptile to metabolize calcium.

The presence of high levels of phosphorus will offset the beneficial aspects of calcium; therefore, the overall diet, including supplements, should provide a minimum of two times more calcium than phosphorus (3:1 in favor of calcium would probably be better).

A variety of methods can be used to heat and light your cages.

Female green anoles often retain light vertebral stripes.

The oxalic acid contained naturally in plants such as spinach and wood sorrel can be at least as detrimental as the phosphorus. Oxalic acid binds with the calcium to form calcium oxalate. Calcium so affected is of no benefit whatever and can even cause kidney damage.

Therefore, the seemingly obvious solution, when natural, unfiltered, sunlight is not available, is to provide a proper and well-rounded diet, vitamin D_3, and calcium supplements.

Don't wait! Once MBD is well advanced, veterinary intervention becomes mandatory and may not be effective. Treatment then involves the use of injectable calcium and immediate diet correction. If the jawbones are too weakened, your lizards may have trouble eating and require

We tend to allow ready availability, rather than common sense, to govern lizard diets. No matter how we strive, it will never be possible for us to feed our captive lizards a fraction of the dietary diversity they would get in the wild—but at least we can try.

force-feeding of a calcium-enhanced soft diet. This treatment is traumatic to the lizard. Prevention is certainly better than treatment.

Articular and Visceral Gout

Symptoms. Swelling of, and difficulty in moving, joints; inflammation and hardening of internal organs.

Diet. Although gout does not appear to occur in insect-eating and omnivorous lizards with the same degree of regularity as with improperly fed herbivorous lizards, it is occasionally reported. Gout is most often related to improper hydration but is now recognized as being diet-related, and perhaps temperature-related as well.

Certain zoo studies have connected gout to temperatures that are not high enough to allow proper and full metabolism of food items. Still, gout seems most commonly reported in herbivorous lizards that are fed moderate to large quantities of animal protein.

Gout has been reported in water dragons, sail-tailed lizards, and basilisks that are fed mostly or entirely on mice. This again points

Even as juveniles, knight anoles are heavy bodied and big-headed.

out how necessary "natural" and varied diets are. In the wild, both water dragons and sail-tailed lizards eat a fair amount of vegetation and a preponderance of insects. Basilisks seem basically insectivorous, although we have had some that have eagerly lapped up honey-fruit mixture and eaten the petals of fresh blossoms. It is probable that only small numbers of nestling mammals and birds are consumed by any of these lizards in the wild.

Gastrointestinal Impactions

Causes. Impactions (blockages) can and do occur in lizards. At times, insufficient gut moisture may cause food items to dry, accumulate, and lead to impaction. Properly hydrated lizards and lizards fed a proper diet are less likely to incur food impactions than lizards kept and fed suboptimally.

Impactions can also be caused by lizards (purposely or accidentally) ingesting stones, dirt, or gravel, dried corncobs, or other such substrate.

Treatment. Each impaction must be assessed individually. Hydration and exercise (especially swimming) may help your lizard to excrete the impaction normally and without intervention; however, some impactions may require mechanical softening or surgery. Consult your veterinarian.

Parasites

Many wild-collected basilisks and most wild-collected water dragons and sail-tailed dragons have endoparasites. Even lizards that are captive-bred and hatched may harbor internal parasites. Thinking about internal parasites has changed. Internal parasites may not be harmful; indeed, with green iguanas at least, they appear to aid in the digestion of the cellulose the iguana ingests. Because of the complexities of identification of endoparasites and the necessity to accurately weigh specimens should an amelioration be deemed necessary, any treatment for internal parasites is best left to a qualified reptile veterinarian.

Endo- (Internal) Parasites

Symptoms. When lizards are stressed by the trauma of capture, shipping, and handling, endoparasites often proliferate, at times to lethal proportions. Be especially vigilant of the weight and overall appearance of newly received, wild-collected, partially aquatic species. Failure to eat, failure to gain weight, or weight loss, may indicate burgeoning parasite loads. Consult your veterinarian for diagnosis and treatment.

Ectoparasites (Ticks and Mites)

Ticks are often found on wild-caught specimens. They are easily removed by first dabbing their body with rubbing alcohol, then, after a few minutes, gently but steadily pulling them free with your fingers or with forceps. There are tick removal devices that are nothing more than gentle tweezers that grasp the tick at its head, and are twirled gently to "unscrew" the mouth parts from the animal's body; these work equally well on dogs and (sigh) humans. Whatever method you use, you want to remove the tick with mouthparts intact. Do not yank the tick off your lizard.

Mites are less of a problem on lizards than on snakes, but they are occasionally encountered. Mites can be seen as tiny pepper-grain-sized

Mites can hide in the smallest of crevices and it is entirely possible for those that remain behind to reinfest your lizard colony.

black specks moving animatedly about on both the lizard and its terrarium. Mites especially favor the wrinkles around eyelids, armpits, and femoral area.

Avoid problems. If you keep lizards in naturalistic terraria (heavily planted terraria with soil, logs, and rocks), it is much easier to quarantine all lizards and eradicate any mites *before* putting the lizards in their permanent terrarium. Mites are more difficult to eradicate if any enter the naturalistic setup.

Should you be unfortunate enough to have mites become established in the naturalistic terrarium, you have several choices. You can introduce *Hypoaspis*, a predatory mite, that preys upon the reptile mite in the caging. You can purchase cultures of *Hypoaspis* from biological supply houses; when the reptile mites are gone, *Hypoaspis* dies out. You can use ProventAMite, which is sprayed in and around the cage after your lizards have been removed to another room. Once the spray has dried, the lizards can be replaced in the cage. You can use Nix head lice control spray in the same manner as ProventAMite, removing the lizard until the spray has dried. A newer product, ReptileRelief, can be sprayed directly on the lizard and in the caging.

The older technique of using pieces of a No-Pest strip (or its generic equivalent) may help to reduce your mite population, but the active ingredient is Vapona, an organophosphate.

To treat lizards in a small terraria, suspend a small piece of a No-Pest strip ($1/2$ inch × 1 inch, [or 12.7–25 mm]) in a wire receptacle (so the lizards cannot come in direct contact with it) from the top of the terrarium for three days. The permanent water source should be removed during treatment. Unlike snakes, which can easily subsist for the three-day treatment period without water, your lizards may be unable to do so. Therefore, we suggest that you replace the cleaned water container in the cage for at least an hour a day, then remove it. If you have anoles or cone-headed lizards that you water by misting, move them to a separate tank and mist them there. Do not allow the No-Pest strip to become wet. After three days, remove the No-Pest, and replace the water container; repeat the process nine days later.

Again—save your lizard from misery while you work to see which mite control system works in your case; quarantine and treat all lizards for mites (or any other malady for that matter) before putting them in a naturalistic vivarium.

In all cases, clean and sterilize as much of the cage and cage furniture as possible; five percent bleach is a good disinfectant. Rinse all items cleaned with bleach thoroughly and let them dry before reusing them. Repeat as necessary.

Trauma-related Maladies

Nose Injuries

Bloodied and bruised noses are commonly seen in the fast-moving basilisks, water dragons, and sail-tailed lizards. These are often initially caused by abrasion in the collecting/shipping containers, and is often worsened by the frightened lizards repeatedly careening into the sides of their terraria/cages. They are, after all, used to much larger ranges. Neosporin or other such antibiotic ointment may prevent infection in the abraded area. Reptile veterinarian Dr. Frederic L. Frye has suggested the use of a liquid bandage (such as Newskin) on seriously injured parts. Left untreated, or if repeatedly reinjured, nose injuries can become infected and progress to mouth rot (infectious stomatitis, literally an infection of the stoma or mouth).

Infectious Stomatitis (Mouth Rot)

Symptoms. Mouth rot is identifiable by the presence of white cheesy (caseous) material on the gums and teeth of the infected specimen. It is most often seen in the proximity of mouth damage. As with all other problems, prevention is always better than cure; before the mouth rot becomes established, eliminate the cause. Use visual barriers such as paper or opaque plastic taped onto tank walls to "warn" flighty species about the limits of their cages.

Although this problem is seldom encountered in anoles, casque-headed lizards, or cone-headed lizards, mouth rot is seen in the larger, nose-rubbing species, such as basilisks, water dragons, and sail-tailed lizards. Fortunately, not every case of bruising or other nose damage results in mouth rot, but when nose damage is recurring and/or hygiene somewhat less than acceptable, mouth rot can occur.

The flight-reactions of many large active adult lizards are deeply ingrained and difficult to impossible to overcome. You should always keep in mind the possibility that you will not be able to tame such a lizard before you make the purchase.

Of the four species of basilisks, the red-headed **Basiliscus galeritus,** *is the least common in captivity. This is a young female.*

Treatment. Bruises and abrasions should be treated as they occur. In many cases, before actual infection has occurred, the simple, periodic, topical application of a good antibiotic (Neosporin, Polysporin, etc.) will usually suffice. If mouth rot has begun, gently remove all loose and affixed caseous material with a diluted Betadine-dipped cotton swab. Use a new swab to dab the infected area with the diluted Betadine. Apply an antibiotic cream.

It is very important that the cause of the abrasions/bruising be removed or corrected. In the case of one huge male red-headed basilisk we once had, we added drapes to his cage—top-to-bottom soft cotton sheeting, hung a few inches inside the back and ends of his cage and covered the front of his cage as well.

We suggest that whenever possible you acquire captive-bred and hatched specimens, or, should this not be possible, that you at least purchase the smaller (and often more easily tamed) lizards.

Broken Bones

Light-bodied arboreal lizards are well adapted to dropping/falling long distances with no problems whatever. Heavier-bodied, more terrestrial species are less well adapted. In captivity, probably because of artificial environments and diets, broken bones can occur. In most cases, it is the leg bones that break. Occasionally there may be a break (or a disarticulation) of the spinal vertebrae. Back injuries are particularly serious and can result in partial or full

The Jamaican giant anole, **Anolis garmani,** *is now a common species in some sections of Miami.*

Often blue in captivity, green basilisks, **Basiliscus plumifrons** *(such as this gravid female), are hobbyist favorites.*

paralysis. In the latter case, euthanasia is recommended. In all cases, even the least serious, veterinary assistance should be immediately sought, and the environment (including the diet) changed/adjusted to prevent recurrence.

Tail Breaks

At last we come to a problem that, although disfiguring, is often not particularly serious. The breaking off (autotomization) of the tail is a predator-avoidance adaptation. Most lizards, like anoles, are capable of such tail loss with little discomfort. Some lizards (perhaps even most, but definitely not all) are capable of tail regeneration. The lizards best adapted for tail autotomization have a weakened area in anywhere from a few to many of the caudal vertebrae. These weakened areas are called caudal planes and are generally in the distal two-thirds of the tail. If the break occurs at one of these areas, regeneration usually begins swiftly. If the break occurs at a point other than a caudal plane, regeneration may be minimal or not occur at all. This is especially true if the break is very close to the body. When occurring at a caudal plane, the break is accompanied by very little bleeding. The area of the break needs only to be kept dry and clean until it dries somewhat. If the break occurs at a point other than at a caudal plane, more bleeding may be evident. Even if it is on the distal half of the tail, veterinary intervention is seldom necessary. Keep the tip dry and clean until it dries.

If the break is near the body, an area where there are usually no caudal planes and that is more highly vascularized, extensive bleeding that requires cauterization and stitching may occur. Seek the advice and services of your veterinarian if the break looks uncomfortable or is in a particularly fleshy area.

Burns

The rather primitive nervous system of a lizard will allow it to come to harm from malfunctioning heating units before the lizard is actually aware of the damage. If all heating equipment in use is regulated and functioning properly, burns seldom occur; however, at some point, malfunctions of regulatory equipment (rheostats/thermostats) may occur, causing your lizards to sustain thermal burns. Inappropriately regulated heat tapes, heating pads, hot rocks, or heating limbs can cause burns to the ventral surfaces of your lizard's body and limbs. The use of these items can also overheat and destroy eggs still in the females' oviducts. Ventral burns may initially appear raw and reddish and may or may not suppurate. As they heal they become rusty-red and either flaky or scabby.

Since, with exception of the little casque-headed lizards of the genus *Corytophanes*, all of the lizards discussed in this book are heliotherms (species that bask in the sunlight), we strongly suggest that you avoid using ventral heaters.

Warmth and illumination are best provided from above for these lizards. Even the little casque-headed lizards, denizens of the shadowy realms of the understory in forested habitats, will thermoregulate in patches of sunlight when necessary, but seem more dependent on the ambient temperatures within their woodland home.

Unshielded overhead bulbs in cages or strong heat lamps positioned too closely above a cage can cause thermal burns to dorsal surfaces of your lizards. Use extreme care when selecting bulb wattage and positioning the lighting unit.

If a burn does occur, immediately correct the malfunctioning implement, adjust the distance between the overhead bulb and the cage top, and treat the lizard's burn with an antibiotic cream.

Overheating (Hyperthermia)

Overly warm temperatures can be as lethal to reptiles as overly cold ones. We suggest that the terrarium/cage temperatures for all of the lizard species discussed in this book be in the 76°F to 82°F (24°C–28°C) range. Providing a warmer basking area will allow the lizards to regulate their body temperature upward if they so desire, and by retreating from the basking area they can again cool themselves.

If your terrarium is glass, a few unexpected minutes of direct sunlight can cause lethal overheating. Be careful where you situate your tank and be aware of the seasonal changes in the position and intensity of the sun's rays.

Initially, overheated lizards are very uncomfortable. They will gape and actively try to escape their quarters. If cooling does not quickly occur, they then become unresponsive and usually undergo a quite considerable change in coloration, with even normally dark specimens often becoming a patchy or pasty gray. If they are still alive when found, cool the lizards immediately in a tub or sink of 72°F to 76°F (22°C–24°C) water. If you've begun this in time, your lizards will live, although they may display neurological problems associated with brain damage. Of course, repositioning or shielding the tank is mandatory.

Overcooling (Hypothermia)

Exposure to cold temperatures can cause many of the same reactions as overheating, but, rather than initially becoming overactive, the affected lizards merely lapse into a state of lethargy, and instead of becoming light in color, they often become dark. Hypothermia most often occurs during the winter in northern climes during power outages or when a lizard escapes from its warmed enclosure into unsuitably heated areas. Although cooling is seldom as quickly fatal as overheating, respiratory ailments are not uncommon following prolonged hypothermia. Warm the lizards in a terrarium of suitable temperature—80°F to 88°F (26.7°C–31°C) or by immersing all but their head in a tub of water that is 80°F to 88°F (26.7°C–31°C), no warmer.

Respiratory Ailments

Unless captive conditions remain poor over a fairly long period of time, most of the lizards discussed in this book are rather resistant to respiratory ailments. Badly stressed wild-collected lizards arriving at the establishments of dealers or hobbyists during the winter may have respiratory ailments, however. Power outages that cause a sharp drop in temperature in humid tanks also cause respiratory problems. Continued maintenance of terrarium temperatures below suitable parameters can be another culprit. A number of different bacteria can be involved in respiratory ailments.

Raise the temperature in your terrarium to 87°F to 90°F (30.5°C–32.2°C) and do not allow the temperature to drop at night. Take your lizard to a veterinarian for further treatment. Isolating the pathogen and determining its sensitivity to specific medications, in case such are needed, is mandatory.

Blister Disease

Although blister disease is not a common malady among anoles, basilisks, water dragons, and allies, it can occur. If forced to remain in contact with a substrate that is too moist or, especially, moist and fouled, or in fouled water, blisters and pustules can appear on the skin. In all but the most advanced cases, progression of this bacterial (or, rarely, bacterial and fungal) disease can be halted by moving the lizards to drier, clean quarters. The blemishes will usually be removed when the lizard next sheds. Shedding sequences are often of increased frequency when blisters (or other skin lesions) are present. In advanced cases, where the lesions reach into body tissues, veterinary treatment must be immediately sought.

BREEDING LIZARDS

Proper conditioning throughout the year, and especially for the few months prior to the breeding season, is of paramount importance if you intend to breed your anole, basilisk, or water dragon.

The conditioning process is every bit as important for captives as for wild-ranging specimens. The reproductive cycles of lizards are triggered by conditions long before the actual breeding season. They include:

• sufficient body weight
• temperature
• rainfall and humidity variations
• photoperiods
• successful brumation or dormancy (if applicable)
• dominance factors, and others, some of which we still don't understand.

Although many of the conditions necessary to breed anoles, basilisks, water dragons, and allied species are similar, there are many slight quirks that must be addressed between groups (sometimes between species).

A sail-tailed anole.

Feeding. When temperatures cool, the metabolism and bodily functions of lizards slow. When temperatures get too cold, bodily functions cease. Thus, when cool, lizards eat less and take longer to digest what they have eaten. Cut back on both the size of the servings and the frequency with which they are offered while your lizards are being cooled in the winter. Hibernating specimens will not, of course, be fed at all.

Anoles may require feeding only every second or third day and water dragons only once or twice a week. Knowing your lizards and their actions and reactions will help immensely during this period. They will tell you when they are hungry.

Egg retention. If conditions within their cage are not suitable for egg deposition, female lizards may be reluctant to lay their clutch. Altering cage conditions so that they are more favorable may induce the female to lay. Such things as deepening the substrate, or altering its moisture content, may be all that is necessary. Providing a feeling of more security for the female by moving the terrarium to a less heavily trafficked area, or by providing a darkened "cave" in which the female can conceal herself during the nesting sequence may help. If the female is still reluctant to lay, an injection of oxytocin or other such hormone may be required. In the most extreme cases (when due to a solidified egg retained from an earlier clutch, or other physical problem, the female is unable to lay), surgical removal of the eggs may become necessary. Consult your veterinarian.

Changes in the shells. Eggs that are viable may discolor somewhat during incubation, but almost never develop "slime," mold, or fungus on their shells. Viable eggs of many lizards that produce parchment-shelled eggs increase noticeably in size during incubation. This size increase allows for the development of the embryo within the shell. Developing eggs may dimple or bulge. This is normal, even with entirely suitable incubating moisture and humidity. However, a noticeable collapse of the shell indicates insufficient moisture in the incubation medium and insufficient relative humidity. If the collapse is noticed quickly enough and the moisture and humidity is raised, the eggs will often continue to develop and hatch perfectly healthy babies.

Age. Both size and age combine to determine a lizard's sexual maturity. Since size is inexorably tied to both the diet and the feeding habits of a lizard, it is very much a variable; however, in general, if properly fed and otherwise cared for, some of the smaller anoles can attain sexual maturity the summer following their hatching.

In our limited experience, cone-headed lizards must be at least 18 months old to breed. Many of the larger basilisks and dragons do not attain sexual maturity until they are 30 months of age or older. This is especially true of the brown water dragon, which virtually ceases to grow during its lengthy periods of winter dormancy. Examples of this species may not reproduce until during their fourth year of life.

Breeding Anoles

Cycling

With the exception of the green anole, which ranges as far northward in the United States as North Carolina and Oklahoma, anoles are a subtropical and tropical group of lizards. It is probable that, among the anoles, it is only the more northerly populations of the green anole that have a period of winter dormancy sufficiently long to be thought of as brumation or hibernation. Certainly other nonequatorial species of anoles are affected by the lowered temperatures and humidity and the shorter hours of daylight during the months of winter. Equatorial anole species are affected by seasonal changes in rainfall, thus ambient humidity.

Neither cool nor dry conditions are the best for egg deposition and incubation, so during the cooler, shorter, and drier days of the year, anoles are comparatively at ease. During this nonreproductive time, males are not quite so agonistic, and both males and females spend more time simply eating and resting (or in periods of dormancy during particularly inclement weather conditions). During this period of relative benevolence and quiescence, wounds are healed, fat reserves are rebuilt, and the lizards—

both males and females—prepare for another season of breeding.

Despite the lack of breeding activity, this period of inactivity is very important to the breeding cycle of an anole; its biological clock is reset, and primed responses are lying in wait.

Onset of breeding season. With the lengthening days of summer, the breeding season of anoles begins in earnest. The days of lethargy are over. The increasing photoperiod induces gonadal recrudescence and, in turn, an increasing hormonal flow. Males begin to again determinedly defend territories. Bobbing bodies and flaring dewlaps are evident. The displays are used to both dissuade nearby competing males from indulging in territory invasion and to entice nearby females, also made receptive by the changing seasons, to visit. Entwined anole bodies are soon followed by females seeking suitable egg deposition sites, and, since many females in a given area nest almost simultaneously, a month and a half later, by myriad baby anoles.

Because they are so common and so inexpensive, anoles as a group receive little attention from herpetoculturists. This is especially true of the green and the brown anoles, both of which are supplied to pet stores as snake food at least as often as for pets.

Breeding in Captivity

To breed even the most common species of anoles in captivity, you will need to replicate, to some degree, seasonal changes.

Temperature and lighting. Here in Florida, in our outside cages, we merely let nature provide heat and lighting. Since even the bottoms of these cages are above the temperature-moderating level of the ground, on extremely cool evenings we provide sufficient heat to

Because they are common and rather easily maintained and bred in captivity, anoles are good lizard pets for beginning herpetoculturists. Breed them, raise them, enjoy them.

keep the cages at 42°F to 48°F (5.6°C–8.9°C) for the green and brown anoles and about 10 degrees warmer for tropical species. Daytime temperatures are also variable, but are usually between 63°F and 80°F (17°C–26.7°C). Sunshine usually is abundant enough during the winter months in Florida to offer the anoles extended opportunities to thermoregulate. The natural photoperiod always prevails.

If an attempt is made to keep indoor lizards at these same low temperatures, the anoles often develop respiratory ailments (see previous chapter). This is just one more indicator that quasi-natural conditions are better than entirely artificial ones; however, anoles kept indoors are not difficult to cycle reproductively. We suggest that the low nighttime temperatures to which your lizards are subjected be warmer. Keeping indoor cages warm would be less of a problem. Suggested winter lows would be 58°F to 65°F (14°C–18°C) for green anoles of northern origin, and 62°F to 68°F (16.7°C–20°C) degrees for those of southern origin and for tropical anole species. The normal daytime temperatures, 83°F to 88°F (28°C–31°C), should be provided. It is important that either an artificially lessened or entirely natural photoperiod be maintained during the winter months. If the anole terrarium is in an often-used room, the terrarium should be draped with a darkening cloth when the room lighting is on in the evening.

Photoperiod. A breach of photoperiod on one or two occasions may make no difference, but if

A young adult knight anole.

it happens regularly it may negate other efforts you are making to sequence the breeding cycle. Photoperiod is very important. During the cooling and lessening of photoperiod, we also reduce humidity. The balancing act you maintain here is critical. Reduced cage humidity will mean that the anoles will need to drink more frequently. And of course, since most anoles are watered by cage misting—well, you get the picture.

During most of the year, we mist the anoles at least twice daily, besides allowing access to all natural showers. During the winter we reduce the mistings to once daily (none on the occasional rainy winter day), but we activate elevated water dishes with water roiled by aquarium air stones. Fortunately, Florida's winter humidity is usually considerably lower than summer humidity, so Mother Nature provides us a helping hand.

The winter regimen should be maintained for 60 to 75 days.

In the early spring we begin allowing nighttime temperatures to increase, upping them by four or five degrees a week for the first two weeks, and bringing them all the way up to the summer norm on the third week. We simultaneously lengthen photoperiod in indoor setups and increase humidity in both indoor and outdoor cages. Soon every anole in the cages is displaying and breeding, and when the anoles have been properly conditioned and have good body weight, the breeding season may last well into the summer months.

Nesting/Egg Laying

The females of many of the smaller species of anoles lay only a single egg at a time, at biweekly intervals. Courtship, but not necessar-

Like most lizards, juvenile Weber's sail-tailed dragons are less colorful than the adults.

ily breeding, occurs prior to each deposition. Little attempt is made by the females to construct a structured nest. Rather, they are basically "egg scatterers" and often just lay the egg on top of leaf-covered moist mulch, in a hollow beneath a tuft of grass, under, or against, the moisture-retaining edge of a fallen limb or piece of debris. More rarely they may scratch out a simple, shallow nest that barely covers the egg. At times, eggs may be laid in plain sight and left. At other times, the female may attempt to scratch debris on top of the egg, or nudge and tamp the egg with her nose until it is more securely hidden in leaves or grass. Some of the larger anoles do dig nests with at least a little more integrity. These anoles, too, lay several clutches a year.

With such cursory nest preparation, it is small wonder that the anoles have evolved to deposit their eggs during the warmest and most humid weather, when climatic and environmental conditions are most favorable to incubation.

Incubation

Anole eggs are durable and easily hatched. Eggs deposited by captive anoles should be removed from the cage for incubation. Do not rotate the eggs on their horizontal axes when you move them. We use margarine containers

> Female anoles will lay their eggs atop the soil and then nose the egg into shelter under a bit of leaf.

Female anoles will use a common houseplant to lay their eggs, if one is available.

or deli cups for egg receptacles. A few pinholes are made in the sides of the cup, and the cups are covered after the eggs are in place inside.

About a dozen eggs may be placed in each cup; the eggs are neither in contact with each other nor the cup sides. The incubation medium can be slightly moistened perlite, vermiculite, sphagnum moss, sand, or sterile potting soil (soils with added fertilizers must be avoided). Sphagnum moss is the medium we prefer, and we use a very unscientific method of preparing it. Whether the moss has been dry packed (such as the kind purchased from nurseries) or is fresh and alive, we wet it thoroughly by soaking it in warm water for a half hour or so. We then empty the water, gather the moss into a ball, and squeeze as much water from it as we can. We then let it sit a while and squeeze it again, even harder. The moss must be only barely moist when the eggs are placed in it.

Also, because they are lightweight and easy to work with, we prefer perlite or vermiculite over sand or soil. If "slightly moistened" is just a little too vague, we can be a little more exacting about the preparation of perlite and vermiculite as an incubation medium than we could about the sphagnum. To prepare both the perlite and vermiculite, we use a ratio of about 1:10, water:perlite/vermiculite by volume. Suggested incubation temperature is between 82°F and 86°F (27.8°C–30°C); this is "room temperature" in Florida. At these temperatures, the eggs of green, brown, and many other small anoles will hatch in 32 to 46 days. A few days longer is usually required for the eggs of the larger species, such as the knight and the Jamaican giant anoles.

Types of incubators. We use either of two kinds. One, the commercially available Hov-a-bator, is available in feed stores or from online sources. Be sure that you get one with adjustable heat, not a bird-egg incubator having a fixed heating temperature.

A home incubator may be constructed from an aquarium and a few odds and ends. It is relatively inexpensive and fairly reliable. The materials needed are:
• an aquarium
• a solid top for the aquarium (a sheet of glass, or even plastic wrap will do)
• a thermostatically controlled submersible aquarium heater
• two bricks
• a plastic shoebox
• an incubating medium (such as perlite, vermiculite, or sphagnum)

Put the aquarium on a stand in a convenient, yet dark and out-of-the-way spot, near an electrical outlet. Put about 3 inches (7.6 cm) of water (enough to cover the heater) in the tank. Most submersible heaters come with a pair of suction cups to hold them in place. Affix the heater to the bottom glass of the tank. Turn the heater on and adjust it to hold the water temperature at about 84°F (28.9°C). Gently put the two bricks, largest flat side down, in the tank, avoiding the heater. Place the shoebox on top of the bricks. Make absolutely certain that the shoebox rests securely and will not tip. Place the cups holding the eggs inside the shoebox.

The shoebox does not need to be covered, but the egg-holding cups do. Place the top on the aquarium. Evaporation and condensation will keep the relative humidity in the closed tank at close to 100 percent. You might wish to adjust the top slightly to lessen the humidity, but not so much that the temperature will vary dramatically (a degree or two variation in either direction will not harm the eggs; more than that might).

Provided the eggs are fertile, the incubation should now be rather uneventful. Hatchling anoles of the smaller forms are extremely small. They will require fruit flies, termites, pinhead crickets, and the tiniest field plankton for not only their first meal, but for several weeks. Hatchling anoles of larger species will willingly accept correspondingly larger food insects.

Breeding Cone-headed and Casque-headed Lizards

Very little is yet known with certainty about the reproductive biology of these basilisk relatives. Of the several species in these two genera, it is the smooth cone-head, *Laemanctus longipes*, which is most commonly bred in captivity. A few zoos and even fewer private hob-

byists have succeeded. Cycling methods used for the tropical anoles have succeeded with these lizards. Of the four breedings at our facility, three clutches numbered three eggs each and one numbered four. Up to five eggs in a single clutch have been reported. The species multi-clutches.

The nests prepared were all only slight depressions and all were constructed amidst the fibrous roots of a small tree only a few inches from the trunk. In one case, after the deposition, the female nudged the eggs into a more compact grouping with her nose and then haphazardly covered them. At 82°F to 86°F (27.8°C–30°C), incubation lasted from 59 to 68 days. The hatchlings, somewhat paler than the adults, were very slender and mostly tail. The snout-vent length was about 1.75 inches (44 mm) and the tail somewhat more than three times that length. The babies proved delicate.

They were reluctant feeders on anything but the smallest of insects, and preferred active baby crickets and grasshoppers over slower-moving insect types. The hatchling *Laemanctus* were also very prone to dehydration, and in the outdoor cages required misting three or four times daily. Once growth began, they seemed hardier, but they continued to be very subject to dehydration.

Although we have kept casque-headed lizards for years, we have never successfully bred them. As a matter of fact, we have never seen any indications of courtship; nor have we been able to find records indicating that any of the casque-headed lizards have been bred elsewhere in America. European hobbyists claim that between 5 and 11 eggs are produced by adult females but have provided no additional information.

A juvenile Philippine sail-tailed dragon.

Breeding Basilisks, Green Water Dragons, and Sail-tailed Dragons

To properly cycle these lizards, the photoperiod should be lessened during the winter months and the ambient temperatures reduced. Nine to ten hours of light will be sufficient. Night temperatures should range from the high 60s°F to very low 70s°F (18.9°C–22°C) and daylight temperatures should be only in the mid- to high 70s°F (24°C–26°C). We suggest that you continue to provide a brilliantly illuminated basking spot with a surface temperature in the low 80s°F (27°C–29°C).

Nests

The lizards in this group usually dig well-formed nests in which to place their eggs, then cover the nests carefully following deposition. Because of this, it is necessary that they be provided suitable deposition areas. A mixture of sand, soil, and peat, sufficiently deep—8 to 12 inches (20–30.5 cm)—and damp enough in consistency so that it will hold the shape of the nest (once dug) is required. The nesting medium can be provided in a deep plastic tub, a plastic terrarium, or even a large and deep plastic flowerpot. Pet green water dragons that have been given the run of a room have been known to jump into large low-hanging planters (suspended flowerpots) and deposit their egg clutch. Because basilisks are even more nimble than water dragons, they can be even more innovative in finding spots to seclude their clutches. Somehow, gravid female basilisks find their ways into what we would have thought to be insurmountable locations to lay their clutches.

Eggs

The eggs of these lizards are fairly large at deposition and increase noticeably in size as incubation progresses. Although the clutch sizes of some larger, older females have been known to number from 16 to 18 eggs, most clutches are much smaller. Clutches of water dragons and sail-tailed lizards usually number from 4 to 12 eggs. The most commonly reported clutch sizes for young females number between 5 and 9 eggs. Basilisks have smaller, and often more, eggs than the various dragons.

Temperatures for Incubating

Various breeders have suggested (and used) differing temperatures for incubating the eggs of basilisks, green water dragons, and sail-tailed lizards. These regimens vary from a constant of 84°F (28.9°C) throughout the entire 60 to 70 days of incubation, to a constant of 88°F (31°C) degrees. Other breeders suggest that the temperature be lowered somewhat, down from 87°F or 88°F (30.6°C–31°C) to 84°F or 85°F (28.9°C–29.4°C). We have learned that it is impossible to argue with success, but suggest that if you do use the 88°F (31°C) regimen, you do so only in a very sophisticated, commercial incubator. Be advised that 88°F (31°C) is very close to the upper lethal maximum for the eggs of many lizard species, and we feel that it gives

no room, whatever, for even the slightest upward climb in temperature. Thermostats and incubators designed for such critical temperature control are much more expensive than any of the units we suggested earlier.

Hatchlings

The hatchlings of most of these lizards are hardy and easily reared.

Although most display decided insectivorous tendencies when babies, all should be offered vegetables and fruits as well as the typical insect fare. Some also enjoy lapping at a honey-fruit mixture (see page 43). Although some breeders recommend getting the hatchlings onto a diet of pinky mice as quickly as possible, it is our belief that a preponderance of mice is a very unnatural diet.

Hatchlings of some (the yellow-striped basilisk, for instance) are so small that fatal dehydration could occur quickly. They must be misted frequently, with a water receptacle available at all times, and provided with a high relative humidity in the cage.

Breeding Brown Water Dragons

Nearly everything said above for the green water dragon applies to this beautiful and interesting species as well. However, brown water dragons, being lizards of more temperate areas, seem to require a period of complete dormancy (brumation/hibernation) during the winter months. Without this, they usually fail to breed at all, and if eggs are produced, they are often inviable. For suggestions on properly hibernating this species, see pages 66–67.

The term *brumation* is now often used in place of hibernation when reptiles are being discussed; actually, the two terms are somewhat interchangeable.

When NOT to Hibernate the Lizards

To cycle reproductively, the brown water dragon seems to require a period of full hibernation. Readying these lizards for this is somewhat complex. First, be aware that unless your brown water dragons are in top condition, they should not be hibernated. A long winter dormancy is both physically and physiologically stressful for even the healthiest of lizards. In nature, many lizards that seem to be in fine condition when they enter hibernation succumb during that period.

Hibernation under captive conditions is no less stressful for a lizard, and may actually be more difficult.

Because hibernation can be fraught with problems, even experienced herpetoculturists seldom subject their reptiles to a lengthy period of complete dormancy unless it is absolutely necessary; therefore, it is suggested that, unless you actually are cycling your brown water dragons for breeding, they not be hibernated.

We also suggest that hatchling specimens not be hibernated during their first winter and that prior to hibernating any specimen of any age, you assure that the lizards are heavy-bodied, healthy, and endoparasite-free.

It is mandatory that the guts of the lizards you intend to hibernate be free from all food materials prior to dormancy.

Digestion shuts down with the cold temperatures necessary for hibernation, and any food left in the gut would putrefy, causing sickness or death. It is equally important that the lizard(s) be adequately hydrated. Keep water available throughout the following sequence:

Technique
• Begin lowering night temperatures and cutting back on feeding two weeks prior to hibernation.
• Hold lowered night temperatures and discontinue feeding ten days prior to hibernation.

A refrigerator with an altered thermostat can be used to hibernate your lizards.

- Be sure photoperiods are also reduced (maximum of ten hours of daylight). A refrigerator with an altered thermostat can be used to hibernate your lizards.
- Begin lowering day temperatures slightly, four days prior to hibernation.
- Again assess the health of the lizards the day prior to placing them in hibernation. Hobbyists in northern climes may choose to merely move the entire terrarium/cage to an unused room, letting the room temperature drop into the mid- to high-50s°F (11.7°C–15°C). The same can be accomplished with greenhouse setups in temperate areas.

In southern Florida, where winter temperatures do not stay sufficiently low for a long enough period, it was necessary for us to make a hibernaculum out of an old refrigerator. We had a refrigerator repairman put a responsive and easily adjustable temperature control switch in line (bypassing the built-in control). Then we preadjusted the refrigerator temperature to 57°F (13.9°C).

Note: Remember that refrigerators are quite efficient at removing moisture from items stored in them. You must carefully monitor the specimens being hibernated in refrigerators to ascertain that they do not become dehydrated.

Facilitating Artificial Hibernation

To facilitate artificial (out of terrarium) hibernation, we placed the brown water dragons, individually, or in twos, in plastic shoeboxes that

Reduce room temperature to 55°F to hibernate all the lizards in a room.

contained an ample amount of fresh, barely moistened sphagnum moss. If the moss is too wet, the lizards can develop blister disease (see page 55). The shoeboxes were then placed in the refrigerator. The lizards were roused (approximately) biweekly and allowed to drink, then placed back in hibernation. We chose to use a 60-day overall hibernating period, and elected to use the months of December and January. Thus, natural photoperiods were still diminishing when the lizards entered hibernation and were on the increase when the lizards were removed.

Upon removal from hibernation, the brown water dragons were returned immediately to a fully warmed and active status. They would often not feed for a day or two, but were soon back to normal activity status—feeding and breeding.

ABOUT ANOLES

Lizards that can change color have always been of interest to humans. Two groups known for this ability are the New World anoles and the Old World chameleons.

There are more than 300 described species of anoles, and quite probably many additional species will eventually be found. Other than differing in adult size, color-changing ability, and habitat preference, the many species of anoles are quite similar. They are long-legged, long-nosed, long-tailed, and rather slender. The males (and the females of some species) have distendable throat fans, which they use to signal other anoles (or humans, if you seem to be on their turf). The toes of most are flattened at the tips and bear transverse lamellae that allow the lizards to climb even vertical smooth surfaces (such as glass) with ease.

The colors and patterns displayed on the throat fans are distinctive for each species. The

Occasionally brown anoles are a rich terra-cotta color.

throat fans of anoles change appearance when viewed by reflected ultraviolet light, turning even the more blasé throat fans of some less colorful species into spectacular displays.

Anoles of several species are collected and sold as feeder lizards or as pets. The brown and the green anole are the species most commonly seen in both categories; however, the Jamaican giant, knight, and crested anoles are becoming more common in the pet trade. All of these types are rather easily kept, even bred, and are fairly long-lived. Longevity of wild-caught adults can range from four to eight years. Now that some species are being captive bred, longevity records of more than a decade can be expected.

Behavior. Male anoles are aggressively territorial, defending their homesites against interlopers. The defended territory of small species is about 4 cubic feet (1.2 m^3). Larger species may claim an entire treetop or several trunks as their defended territory. Males defend their perceived territory by compressing their body to appear larger, doing push-ups and head bobs and distending the throat fan. A low vertebral ridge may also be elevated. If this does not dissuade the interloper, the defending lizard will then sidle broadside toward the interloper, then dart toward and actually skirmish with the offender. The fights can be fierce, and will last until the interloper rushes off or the defender is deposed.

Diet. Although anoles are predominantly insectivorous, they may also lap nectar, pollen, or tree saps, and have been seen drinking sugar water from hummingbird feeders. Captives readily drink the honey-fruit mixture described on page 43, but this cannot be their entire diet. Large species are the more omnivorous and may occasionally eat berries, figs, or brightly colored flower petals.

Reproduction. Anoles are oviparous. From late spring throughout the summer, the female lays a single egg (small species) to 2 or 3 eggs (large species) at fortnightly intervals. Each incidence of ovarian development is stimulated by a courtship sequence. Since sperm can be stored in viable condition for periods exceeding eight months, actual copulation prior to each egg deposition is not essential. If a nest is prepared, it is a rather haphazard affair. A shallow scrape only slightly deeper than the diameter of the egg may be made in moist ground. As often as not, the egg is merely placed in leaf litter, amid trash heaps, or in similar moisture-retaining sites. Incubation averages two months. It may be somewhat less in hot weather, somewhat greater if climatic conditions are cool. Hatchlings are relatively large.

Anoles in the United States

The several color-changing species of anoles, including the giant species, are canopy dwellers. Although the non–color-changing brown species are perfectly capable of climbing, they are more at home on the trunks of trees, in shrubs, or even on the ground, than in the canopy.

Color-changing Anoles

The green anole, *Anolis carolinensis*, is native to the southeastern United States. It is our only native anole. The green anole is a small lizard, with an adult size of about 6 to 7 inches (15–17.8 cm). It is found throughout the Gulf Coast states, Georgia, the southern half of North Carolina, all of South Carolina, southeastern Tennessee, southeastern Oklahoma, and southern Arkansas. It is also found in Hawaii, in the Mexican state of Tamaulipas, and has become established in Japan. The green anole is a highly arboreal woodland edge, pine-palmetto scrubland, cypress swamp, and backyard lizard.

When cool, basking green anoles are brown, a color that quickly absorbs heat. When warm, if in the open, the lizards are often a pale green; in the shade they may remain brown. If active, green anoles are often just that, a bright green. If involved in aggression, they are green but have a black patch behind each eye. A lighter vertebral line is often present. This may appear zipperlike on females. Males are slightly larger than the females, and their tail base is heavier. The throat fan in the female is nonexistent to vestigial. Over most of the range, the male's throat fan is usually a pale pink. Some males in south Florida have white or pale cream throat fans.

The Cuban green anole, *Anolis porcatus,* is now established in the vicinity of Miami, Florida. Although genetically distinct, it is so similar in appearance and size to the native green anole that the two species are easily mistaken. Rely on your supplier for the identification of this species.

The Hispaniolan green anole, *Anolis chlorocyanus,* is tenuously established in and near Miami, Florida. Males attain a length of 9 inches (22.9 cm); females are somewhat smaller. This pretty and wary anole has a cobalt blue dewlap. The dewlap is present on both sexes but is much smaller on the female. The tail scalation consists of whorls of small and large scales.

Color-Changing Giant Anoles

Two giant anole species, the knight anole, *A. e. equestris,* and the Jamaican giant anole, *A. garmani,* are established in extreme southern Florida.

The Knight Anole

This Cuban native has been present in Florida for about four decades.

Size. Not only is the knight anole the largest species found in Florida, it is the largest anole in the world. Adult males may slightly exceed 18 inches (45 cm) in length; the females are somewhat smaller.

Appearance. Although the knight anole is usually a brilliant green color, it is well capable of taking on a deep brown hue. In all colors, two light yellow-to-white flash marks are visible. The one on the shoulder is the most prominent, but the second, paralleling the upper lip from eye to ear opening, will also be discernible. Widely spaced, contrastingly colored crossbars are also occasionally present. Intersti-

Green anoles can change color from bright green to deep brown. The color-changing abilities of the green anole are well known. An individual lizard may be brilliant green one minute and deep brown the next. The mechanisms that trigger these changes include stress, temperature, humidity, and light intensity.

tial (between scale) skin is colored differently than the scales. When visible, this may create a reticulated pattern of contrasting colors. The rear of the knight anole's head is more heavily casqued, and its head proportionately larger than that of any other U.S. anole species. This is a truly impressive lizard species. The throat fans are present on both sexes. The fan of the male is of tremendous size, reaching from the anterior lower lip to well back on the chest. The fan of the female is proportionately smaller.

Behavior. Knight anoles are highly arboreal, usually keeping well up in the canopy during cool weather, but descending to the trunks below the canopy when temperatures are high. During midsummer, knight anoles may descend to only a few feet above ground, where they often assume a head-down resting/hunting position on the tree trunks. Although knight anoles seem to prefer exotic foliage trees, we have also seen them on palms.

When threatened, knight anoles may stand their ground and can bite painfully hard. Typically, before biting, a knight anole will present itself broadside to the source of its displeasure, laterally flatten its body, open its mouth, extend its immense dewlap (at least somewhat), and erect a prominent nape and anterior vertebral crest.

Patchy green and brown coloration on the green anole may indicate stress or simply an impending color change.

The Jamaican Giant Anole

The Jamaican Giant Anole, *Anolis garmani*, is the rarer of the two giant species in Florida. Adult males are often near a foot (30.5 cm) in overall length. The females are somewhat smaller.

Both sexes of the Jamaican giant anole have throat fans. That of the male is large, of a yellow coloration and may or may not have an orangish center. The throat fan of the female is proportionately smaller and of a darker coloration. The pale dewlaps contrast strikingly with the usual bright green body color. Jamaican anoles have

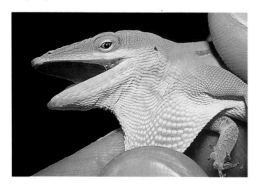

a low crest of enlarged serrate scales down their back and a more prominent nuchal (nape) crest. Displaying males not only slowly distend, then retract the large throat fan, but through muscular contractions may elevate the vertebral crest more prominently as well.

Non–Color Changing Anoles

Just as the color-changing anoles are difficult to differentiate from one another, several of the non–color-changing (brown) anoles are quite similar to each other in appearance. Dewlap color and size is often the most significant differentiating feature.

The Brown Anole

The brown anole, *A. sagrei* ssp., of Cuba and the Bahamas is now firmly established in the southeastern United States. It is particularly abundant in peninsular Florida. This hardy and

The dewlap color of the pale-throated green anole, **Anolis carolinensis seminolus** *(of southern Florida), varies from white to gray.*

Bark anoles may be brownish gray or pea green but are never bright green.

The Cuban green anole is very similar to our native species but has a proportionately longer snout and may display blue or gold spotting on the sides.

Size, facial markings, and the shape of the dewlap help distinguish A. equestris (above) from Anolis carolinensis (below).

successful alien species occurs in high population densities near human habitations as well as in open scrubland and woodland. It can be seen nodding and bobbing among grasses, on sidewalks, and from clearing edges, as well as from brush piles, heaps of building debris, or from low on the trunks of trees and shrubs. When frightened, rather than darting for the nearest tree, it darts into or beneath any available cover.

Appearance. Male brown anoles are much larger of the two sexes both in length and proportionate heaviness of body. Males approach the length of 8 1/2 inches (21 cm). They are also the darker of the two sexes and usually lack all but traces of the dark-edged, scalloped, or straight middorsal stripe so typical of the juveniles and females. The throat fan of the males may vary from yellow-orange to orange and has a whitish border. When not distended, the border of the throat fan forms a light streak on the throat of the male lizard.

Some males have rather well-developed tail crests. Erectile nuchal crests are well developed and a vertebral crest slightly less so.

Large-headed Anole

This impressive yellow-dewlapped anole has been established in southern Florida in small colonies for several decades.

The large-headed anole is marginally the largest in body bulk of Florida's introduced brown-colored anoles. Adult males are a rather heavy-bodied 8-inches (20 cm) in length.

Appearance. The vernacular name "large-headed" refers only to cranial size of the adult males of this Hispaniolan native. The heads of the females and the juveniles are not enlarged.

Always of some shade of brown, occasionally vague olive overtones are present. This anole is darkest dorsally. Males have both a dorsolateral and a lateral stripe. Both are narrow and light (sometimes only vaguely visible), and they tend to converge posteriorly. The dorsolateral band is often broken into a series of spots. The contrast between dorsal and lateral colors seems the least when the animals are cool. A series of about a half-dozen dark crossbands may or may not be visible. If present, the crossbands may either terminate at, or be interrupted by, the contrastingly colored lateral stripe. The very large throat fan of the male, yellow to buff in coloration, may shade to pale orange centrally when distended.

Males are capable of erecting vertebral and nuchal crests; the nuchal crest can be especially prominent.

Female large-heads are very similar in appearance to the females of the ubiquitous brown anole, being brown to reddish-brown (lighter laterally), with a dark-edged light ver-

Although bark anoles are often offered in the pet trade, they are not an easily kept species. The preferred diet of various ant species is difficult to replicate in captivity. We consider the several subspecies of this anole poor candidates for herpetoculture.

tebral stripe. This stripe may be either straight or irregularly edged. Females also retain the light lateral stripes and often display one or two pairs of small, light shoulder spots, the anterior pair being the more discernible.

Adult males display while positioned head down on a prominent trunk or post. The pale but reflective dewlaps of displaying males resemble the motions of a host of tiny semaphores.

Diet. Besides the normal diet of insects, this big-headed species will accept tiny terrestrial snails.

The Bark Anoles

The smallest of the anole species of the United States is the diminutive *A. distichus* ssp. Because the inconspicuous colors and patterns blend remarkably well with the bark of the trees on which they are found, these 4$\frac{1}{2}$-inch-long (11 cm) lizards are aptly named.

Appearance. Bark anoles are the smallest species of anole to become established so far in the United States. The pale yellow dewlap of the males and the dark dorsal chevrons of both species are distinguishing characteristics. Both color and pattern of these interesting little anoles are variable and provide the lizards with remarkable camouflage. Usually there is a series of dark chevrons (apices rearward) dorsally, a dark bar between the eyes, and a pair of light spots at the rear of the head. Occasional males

are a rich pea (but never bright) green. The tail and limbs of all races are prominently banded. The splay-legged scuttlings of this species are also somewhat different from the movements of other anoles.

The Crested Anole

Anolis cristatellus is native to Puerto Rico. It has been established in Miami-Dade County for several decades.

These lizards have three crests: caudal (tail) crest, vertebral (body), and nuchal (nape) crests. The nuchal and vertebral crests are voluntarily erectile through muscle contractions. The caudal crest; always at least vaguely discernible on adult males, is the one for which they are named.

Appearance. A brown lizard, males have well-defined tail bands and may or may not have body blotches.

The large throat fan of the male is pale yellow. Females look much like the more ubiquitous brown anole, having a dark-edged light vertebral stripe.

Like many other anoles, the crested often positions itself rather low on tree trunks and fence posts in a head down position. Male crested anoles, the only sex with the crest, attain a length of slightly more than 7 inches (17.8 cm). The females are much smaller.

Several other anoles from the West Indies and from Central America are occasionally offered for sale. The care of all is similar to those mentioned above.

Bark anoles are persistently arboreal and, although usually seen low on the trees, ascend rapidly if disturbed.

Because most of these lizards— basilisks and their relatives and water dragons and their relatives—are large, fast, and active, most will require disproportionately larger enclosures than members of the anole family.

The adults of the true basilisks and the water dragons all attain 2 feet (61 cm) or more in length, and should be maintained in terraria or caging of not less than 50 gallons (189 L) in size. Caging of at least twice this size (and preferably larger) would be far better.

The smaller basilisk relatives—the casque-headed and the cone-headed lizards—are smaller, naturally less active, and much less frenzied in their escape and avoidance responses than the true basilisks. Because of this, the casque-heads and the cone-heads may be maintained much like the anoles, in cages that are smaller proportionately to the overall size of the lizards.

To determine the preferred habitats of these lizards, consider their colors and body proportions—and envision a tree. For the basilisk family members—Corytophanidae—the green(ish), lightly built cone-headed lizards (*Laemanctus*) are the canopy dwellers. On the trunks, near the forest floor, are the brown cryptically colored

The common casque-headed lizard.

and shaped casque-headed lizards (*Corytophanes*). The heavy-bodied basilisks (*Basiliscus*) are found basking on horizontal branches at low to moderate heights, over quiet waters. This last area is shared by the water dragons (*Physignathus*) and sail-tailed dragons (*Hydrosaurus*), members of the family Agamidae.

The green basilisk of the New World and the green water dragon of the Old World are associated with overgrown, evergreen areas. While the brown basilisk and the brown water dragon may occur in forested areas, they are more typically creatures of open, deciduous scrub.

The basilisks, water dragons, and sail-tailed dragons are all typically associated with water courses or water holes and do not hesitate to enter water and submerge in efforts to evade predation. When frightened while on the ground, virtually all of the lizards in these genera (including the casque-headed and cone-headed lizards) run bipedally. Their hind legs are strong and can carry them quickly from real or perceived threats, sometimes even across water.

Although the sail-tailed dragons—in most ways Old World ecological equivalents of the New World basilisks—have broadened toes, they have not yet shown an ability to run on water. Since they are fast, however, we would not be surprised if, under ideal conditions, they would be able to do so.

Diet. To the best of our knowledge, the two small members of the basilisk family—the cone-headed and casque-headed lizards—are predominantly insectivorous. However, it was not uncommon for us to find the cone-headed lizards eating heartily from the honey-fruit mixture (see page 43) containers positioned near the top of their cages. These pureed mixtures were provided basically for the cagemates of the cone-heads, the Malagasy day geckos, but were used extensively by the anoles as well.

The cone-heads would also nibble the petals from freshly picked hibiscus blossoms that we placed among the leaves in the top of their *Ficus* tree. We have not yet seen the little casque-headed lizards partake of vegetable materials, but these lizards are so secretive that

it would not be difficult to overlook them doing so. Certainly, if the casque-heads were to partake of the honey-fruit mixture, it would be from receptacles positioned lower in the cage (but probably not on the bottom) amidst the denser foliage.

The larger lizards—the true basilisks, water dragons, and sail-tailed dragons—eat insects of most kinds voraciously, but also readily feed on suitably sized mice (from "pinkies" to "jumpers," depending on the size of the lizards), canned dog foods, the honey-fruit mixture, blossoms, and some fresh fruits and vegetables.

The food insects included gut-loaded crickets and king mealworms, butterworms, waxworms, nonnoxious caterpillars, and June and other similar beetles. The fruits and vegetables included dark lettuces (leaf, romaine, escarole, etc.), some banana, apricots, peaches, grated apple, grated squash, dandelion greens and flowers, hibiscus leaves and flowers, nasturtium leaves and flowers, and many kinds of berries.

Water. This is important to all living creatures and is garnered in many differing ways. Our cone-headed and casque-headed drink their fill of droplets immediately following a cage sprinkling. They are also most active during or immediately following a light rain shower or a light misting from the hose. Heavy showers or heavy sprinklings will usually render the lizards inactive. The cone-heads will drink the individual droplets from the uppermost foliage, gingerly moving from drop to drop as if knowing instinctively that undue branch and leaf motion would cause many droplets to fall before they were reached by the lizards.

The water-loving sail-tailed dragon will soak if its water dish is large enough.

The casque-headed lizards, on the other hand, seemed to prefer to lick the water as it ran down the inner, vertical trunks of the *Ficus*, to which they usually clung. We found that correctly positioning one (or several) freshly filled drip bucket(s) above the tree would induce longer periods of drinking by the casque-heads than short mistings.

Although the larger, partially aquatic basilisks, water dragons, and sail-tailed dragons eagerly lap up the pendulous droplets left on foliage by rain showers and mistings, they are less dependent on this method of drinking to retain suitable hydration than their smaller relatives. The three genera of larger lizards will readily drink from their containers of water. In the case of these larger lizards, the water container should be large enough for the lizard(s) to sit comfortably in. Because these lizards frequently defecate while in their water (indeed, entering the water seems to stimulate them to defecate), care must be taken that the water is changed as often as necessary. If several lizards are caged together, this can be very often.

In the wood-bottomed, outside cages that we used (and that can be used in most areas of the country during the summer months), keeping the water clean was a snap. The containers we use were the largest plastic kitty litter pans available. Fortunately, these have a prominent lip. With a small saber saw we cut a panel from the wooden cage bottom slightly smaller than the top of the water pan to be used. When properly cut, the pan can be inserted and will be suspended by its lip. We then drilled a hole for a large hard rubber stopper in the bottom of the water pan, stoppered it, and filled the pan with fresh water. The plug could be pulled as often as necessary, the container swabbed

> Dirty water is an ideal avenue for parasite and pathogen transference between specimens. Keeping your lizard's water clean and fresh at all times is of paramount importance.

with a disinfectant, rinsed well, restoppered, and refilled. Each cleaning took only a few minutes. Although cleaning water is usually far more inconvenient in inside cages, we got around part of the problem by having a drain installed in the floor of our attached greenhouse. After this was done, we could easily dispose of the water once the pan was removed. Sterilizing, rinsing, and refilling also became easier when a small hose was used.

The Basilisks, Casque-headed, and Cone-headed Lizards

There are only 3 genera (9 species) in the family Corytophanidae. This breaks down to four species in the genus *Basiliscus*, the basilisks; three species of *Corytophanes*, the casque-headed lizards (often called "forest chameleons" or "helmeted iguanids"); and two species of cone-headed lizards of the genus *Laemanctus*.

All members of this family are oviparous (egg laying). All have some sort of head adornment. All are of Latin American distribution. All are lightly built with long limbs. All are agile climbers; in fact, the *Laemanctus* are canopy species.

Basilisks and cone-headed lizards bask frequently and often for long periods, especially during periods of cool weather or when relative humidity is low. Casque-headed lizards are less apt to bask, depending instead on suitably warm ambient temperatures being maintained at all times.

Laemanctus longipes, the Central American cone-headed lizard, has very long legs and hops rather than runs.

These lizards like high humidity. High relative humidity is maintained in the cage by providing a sizable but shallow water dish as well as by periodic spraying (outside cages) or misting (inside cages). Growing plants also increase humidity in cages.

The Basilisks

The basilisks are veritable speedsters and excellent swimmers. When moving rapidly, they are bipedal. The large hind foot of the basilisk, in combination with long rear toes that bear a slight flange, provide a comparatively great surface area. Due to these specializations, the young (and to a lesser degree, some larger specimens) basilisks are capable of running across the surface film of quiet waters; however, if they slow or stop, they sink.

Within their natural Latin American range, the ability to "walk on water" gives rise to another common name for the basilisks, the "Jesus Christ" lizard.

Appearance. All four species within the genus *Basiliscus* have some degree of cranial cresting as well as gular pouches. Additionally, some basilisks have vertebral and/or caudal crests. The adornments are invariably better developed on males than females. The males of the basilisks are much longer and bulkier than the females.

Basilisks are frequently encountered resting quietly on the diagonal or horizontal branching of low shrubs that are in the proximity of water. Pond- and marsh-edge locations are favored. In Mexico, we have found *Basiliscus vittatus* very abundant in disturbed areas. On the occasions that we have stayed at hotels with non-enclosed swimming pools, the basilisks along the pool edge may considerably outnumber the often squeamish tourists.

When they are frightened, basilisks either dive into the water or rely on a headlong flight to escape. They are fast and wary.

Diet. The basilisks are insectivorous but will also add a nestling bird or baby rodent to their diet. In captivity, some will also eat canned dog food. They may also nibble on blossoms and some fresh fruits and vegetables.

In captivity, all will adapt to large well-planted terraria; outdoor step-in caging seems to be even better. Tropical daytime temperatures (85°F to 95°F, or 29.5°C–35.0°C) and high humidity are needed.

The Green Basilisk

The members of the genus *Basiliscus* are frequently seen in captivity, and of the four species of basilisks, the hands-down favorite is the very beautiful green basilisk, *B. plumifrons*. Not only is this species the most brilliantly colored, but the males are the most prominently adorned of the four as well.

Adult males of the green basilisk have finlike crests on the back and tail and a double crest on the head. It is from the narrow, plumelike anterior cranial crest that the vernacular "plumed basilisk" and specific name of *plumifrons* is derived.

The ground color is green (varying from light to dark), often with blue lateral spots and some vertical black markings in the vertebral crest. The iris is brilliant orange-yellow. Adult males attain a length of more than 28 inches (71 cm). Adult females are several inches smaller.

We must reiterate that basilisks can be nervous lizards that, if startled, may dash into the sides of the terrarium, sometimes resulting in severe nose (rostral) damage (see Nose Injuries, page 51). Wild-collected lizards tend to be more nervous than captive-bred and -hatched specimens. Males are often more nervous than females. It may be necessary to cover most of

The Central American cone-headed lizard is an agile arborealist.

the glass of a basilisk terrarium with an opaque paper (or other such material) to prevent frightening the lizards.

The green basilisk is a species of forest pool, marsh, and swamp edges. It ranges from Guatemala to Costa Rica.

Until recently, green basilisks have been only sporadically available to the pet trade. Currently, however, not only are large numbers of these lizards being collected and imported from Nicaragua, but captive breeding successes are now providing large numbers of hatchlings to hobbyists.

Dietary studies are still needed for this species. Despite the fact that they live well and are rather easily bred, there is a noticeable tendency for captive-bred green basilisks to be duller—less intensely green—than those from the wild. Perhaps a higher concentration of beta-carotenes would reverse this trend.

Basilisks need large caging; if you cannot provide this, seek a smaller lizard species.

Basiliscus plumifrons is a showy creature, combining color, head casque, and vertebral and caudal crest.

Although the species does not yet seem to be established in Florida, several green basilisks of both sexes have now been collected along Miami, Florida canals. All those we have seen looked like escaped or released wild-collected imports. All have healed but still noticeable rostral injuries or other disfigurements would have reduced their value in the pet trade.

The Two Brown Basilisks

B. basiliscus and *B. vittatus* are both a brown ground color. Both have wide yellow to white dorsolateral stripes and well-separated dark dorsal crossbars. *B. basiliscus* (Costa Rica to Colombia and Venezuela) has a well-developed (high) cranial as well as both vertebral and caudal crests. The adult males of both attain about 2 feet (61 cm) in overall length; the females are smaller.

The head crest of *B. vittatus* is triangular, the vertebral crest is low, and the caudal crest represented by only a keel. This latter species occurs from Mexico southward to Costa Rica and is now firmly established along the canal systems of extreme southern Florida. It is not as flamboyantly adorned as its more southern relative, but *B. vittatus*, which we will call the northern brown basilisk, is a pretty and alert lizard. A horizontal shoulder stripe of the brightest yellow offsets the otherwise brown coloration nicely.

Although the specimens of this interesting lizard supplied to the pet trade of the United States are largely wild collected, they are no longer imported from Latin America in any great numbers. Rather, the pet industry specimens are now collected from canal-bank and canal-side vegetation in Dade County, Florida, where the species is now common and seemingly on the increase. Because of its ready availability to American hobbyists, the northern brown basilisk is seen in greater numbers in the American pet trade today than it ever was when the trade depended on imported specimens. Also, the domestically collected specimens now available are less stressed than the imports were.

Both the northern and southern brown basilisks have now been bred in captivity.

The Red-headed Basilisk

The coveted—but very infrequently seen—red-headed basilisk, *B. galeritus*, of Ecuador and Colombia, has a well-developed cranial crest, but the vertebral and caudal crests are represented by a series of enlarged flattened scales, each separated from the next by several small scales. The ground color of this pretty lizard is russet. Olive-green highlights are present on the head and anterior trunk. Despite high prices, this lizard sells readily on the rare occasions when it is offered in the American pet market.

The red-headed basilisk is a nervous and easily stressed lizard. If you are ever fortunate enough to acquire a pair, they will need a large cage with many visual barriers in an area of your house where foot traffic is minimal. Red-headed basilisks do not take well to even the most careful handling. This is easily seen by the loss of color that occurs when the lizards are restrained. Bert and Hester Langerwerf of Agama International have found that even the hatchlings of the red-headed basilisk are more delicate and easily stressed than the babies of any other basilisk species. Unlike the babies of the green and brown basilisks, which can be easily raised in communal terraria, babies of the red-headed basilisk fare poorly unless in an individual terrarium.

Basilisks can be differentiated by the size and shape of the head plumes.
A. Basiliscus vitattus, B. B. plumifrons, C. B. galeritus, and D. B. basiliscus.

Casque-headed Lizards

There are three lizard species in this genus, but only one, *Corytophanes cristatus*, the common casque-headed lizard, is seen with any frequency.

In contrast to the rather smooth appearance of the common casque-head, the spiny casque-headed lizard, *Corytophanes hernandesi*, has isolated, elongate, spinous scales over the front portion of the upper body. The occipital ridges or crests are separate from the cranial crest.

The third species, *C. percarinatus*, is unknown in herpetoculture. It has keeled scales on the crown of the head, and the occipital ridges do not extend anteriorly much beyond the cranial crest.

Range. The common casque-head is found from southern Mexico to Colombia. The spiny casque-head is from Central Mexico to

Guatemala, while *C. percarinatus* is from Oaxaca, Mexico, to El Salvador.

Appearance. Common casque-headed lizards are smooth-skinned, attractive creatures that are cryptically colored in earthen tones and that have variable light and/or dark bars. A distinct gular pouch is present. The occipital ridges are continual, with the canthi rising and nearly converging at the front of the very high and full cranial crest. A line of serrate scales, extending to the base of the tail, represents the vertebral crest.

Although an arboreally adapted forest species, these lizards prefer to remain in the understory. We have found them on the ground standing upon fallen leaves, on the horizontal trunks of fallen trees, and three feet or lower on the trunks of standing trees.

Behavior. *Corytophanes* has a curious method of escaping detection. At first, when startled, it

Despite their quiet demeanor, casque-headed lizards do not enjoy being handled.

The "plumes" on the head of this adult male green basilisk are fully developed.

may move away in a series of sporadic, froglike hops. Facing a predator such as a snake, it will turn its body broadside to the snake and flatten itself vertically, making itself look much larger than it actually is. If further frightened, it often becomes almost catatonic. It stiffens its body, tips its head downward, closes its eyes, and remains in that position for long periods. Once quiescent, the lizard virtually disappears against the fallen leaves of its woodland home.

When grasped, even gently, a casque-headed lizard will stiffen and go into its catatonic-like state. If it becomes necessary to move or to otherwise handle a casque-head, let the lizard crawl up onto your hand. It will usually sit quietly on your hand or on a short section of suitably thick limb without physical restraint.

Corythophanes are difficult to acclimate, and should be considered delicate captives. They may be maintained in small groups of one male and one to three females, seemingly with no stress. Although ours are maintained for most of the year in sizable, heavily planted, walk-in cages, their quiet demeanor enables keepers to consider much smaller cages for these humidity-loving lizards.

The shade-dwelling casque-headed lizards do not bask frequently. In their forestland homes, ambient temperatures are usually entirely suitable for optimum activity and body functions. In our Florida location, the walk-in cages were maintained outside and unheated at all times, except during the passage of winter cold fronts. In the winter we affixed Pliofilm to the outside of the

The northern brown basilisk, **Basiliscus vittatus,** *is the species most common in captivity.*

cages as a windbreak. Heat was provided when nighttime temperatures dipped into, or below, the low 50s°F (10°C–12°C), but even during periods of comparative cold, our casque-heads seldom basked. A high humidity was always maintained in the cages, and during the hottest days of summer, the cage was sprayed several times daily or an overhead watering pail was utilized.

Size. Adult males may barely exceed 12 inches (30.5 cm) in total length, with females being marginally smaller.

Diet. These lizards are insectivorous, but the exact variety of their diet in the wild is as yet undetermined. They seem to be wait-and-ambush feeders, feeding on whatever insects stroll past them. Their diet in the wild may include ants. In captivity, feed dusted and gut-loaded crickets, and field plankton when possible.

Breeding. Casque-headed lizards are not currently captive bred in any great numbers. As a matter of fact, of the half dozen small clutches of eggs that our females have produced over the years, only three eggs, one in one clutch and two from another, were fertile. Since we had never seen the adults copulate, we were actually surprised that any eggs were fertile. The hatchlings were about 3.5 inches (8.9 cm) in total length. Of this, more than 50 percent was tail length. The cresting was poorly developed. The hatchlings did not survive. We know of no other captive breedings (and, indeed, our meager success could have been due to sperm retention rather than on-site breeding). Thus, with virtually no captive breeding known, the pet industry is entirely dependent on wild-collected imported specimens.

Cone-headed Lizards

The two species of cone-headed lizard, genus *Laemanctus*, bridge the gap between the speedy basilisks and the catatonic casque-headed lizards.

Of the two species of *Laemanctus*, it is usually *L. longipes* that is available in the pet trade. This species, present from southern Mexico to Nicaragua, has a smooth posterior edge to the conelike cranial casque. The cranial casque of the Mexican *L. serratus* is prominently serrate along its posterior rim.

Appearance and behavior. Although some researchers describe *Laemanctus* as being terrestrial, we have found them to be persistently arboreal. The cone-heads are alert predators of canopy insects. There, their greens and tans render the lizards virtually indiscernible. The cone-heads lack vertebral or caudal cresting, having only the flat-topped ridge at the back of their heads as adornment. This is equally developed in both sexes.

Both species of these lizards have tails three or more times the combined length of their head and body. Adults measure up to 18 inches (45.7 cm) overall. Hatchlings measure about 7 inches (17.8 cm) in total length, of which all but 1.75 inches (4.5 cm) is tail.

Specimens in our walk-in cages spend most of their time in the crowns of the small *Ficus* trees that grow in the 6-foot-tall (183 cm) enclosures.

Cone-heads are usually quite inactive but are capable of bursts of considerable speed. When pressed, they are able to jump rather nimbly from leafy branch to leafy branch in escape efforts. Their long hind legs give them a somewhat ungainly appearance, belying the actual agility of the lizards.

Diet. Our lizards eagerly accepted vitamin-dusted crickets that climbed to their "canopy" home and would even more eagerly leap in acrobatic attempt to snatch flying moths from the air. Even within the constraints of the cage, the lizards seldom missed.

Hatchlings fed more reluctantly, needing tiny feed insects and absolute quiet before they would accept their first few meals. Hatchlings are very prone to dehydration, but once they begin feeding they are no more delicate than the hatchlings of most lizards.

The cone-heads of all sizes, but especially the hatchlings, are reluctant to drink water from a dish, even when the water is stirred by an aquarium air stone. However, all of the lizards drink water droplets from the foliage when the cage is sprayed or misted or, outside, during periods of natural rainfall.

Breeding. Several hobbyists and zoos have bred these lizards. The females multi-clutch each year, laying one to three eggs per deposition.

Although both species of cone-headed lizards have a reputation for being delicate, it is primarily dehydration the makes them so. Internal parasites are often a secondary problem. In concert the two problems can quickly be devastating. If newly acquired *Laemanctus* are promptly rehydrated, they will often live for years.

Water Dragons and Sail-tailed Dragons

The water dragons, *Physignathus*, and the closely allied sail-tailed dragons of the genus *Hydrosaurus* are beautiful and, if properly stabilized, hardy lizards of moderate size. Usually considered less nervous than basilisks, the difference can be marginal when wild-collected

> You will have better success taming, or at least quieting, a young lizard than an adult.

adult specimens are involved. And, if a degree of nervousness can be assigned, we would have to say that the sail-tailed lizards are usually more flighty than the water dragons.

When newly collected, wild-caught specimens of either water or sail-tailed dragons are received, unless great care is taken to prevent it, they will soon have their noses bruised and bloodied from continued escape attempts. Sometimes this will happen no matter what precautions are taken, but in general, secure, stress-free quarters will help you attain initial success with all of these lizards.

In all cases, whenever it is possible, we suggest that you begin your relationship with these lizards by acquiring captive-hatched specimens. If these are not available, hold out for immature wild-collected specimens.

In fact, wild-collected adult specimens of the various sail-tailed dragons may never become tame, no matter how much effort you expend, and taming some wild-collected adult water dragons may prove only slightly less difficult.

Water Dragons

Unlike the anoles, basilisks, and their relatives, which are of exclusively New World distribution, the two species of water dragons, genus *Physignathus*, are just as exclusively Old World. They are members of a huge family, the Agamidae. Actually, although two species are currently contained in the genus, it is likely that one, the Australian brown water dragon, will soon be reclassified. Researcher Scott Moody has found that the brown water dragon is more closely allied to the sail-tailed dragons of the genus *Hydrosaurus* than to its green relative. It seems probable that a new genus will be created for the brown water dragon.

The Green Water Dragon

Water dragons are hardy, magnificent lizards of moderate size. Both are now being extensively bred in captivity, but wild-collected specimens of the Southeast Asian green water dragon, *P. cocincinus*, continue to be imported to both America and Europe in large numbers. Prices for the green water dragon reflect this ready availability of wild specimens, deflating the prices of even captive-bred specimens. Adult imported green water dragons may sell today for as little as $25; captive-bred hatchlings might be a little more. On the other hand, the brown water dragons, an endemic Australian species, are protected and not currently imported by the pet trade in any great numbers. Although less colorful than the green, the relative rarity of the brown water dragon insures that they seldom sell for less than $150 each. Again, captive-bred and -hatched brown water dragons are usually somewhat more expensive than the few imported specimens.

The two species of water dragon are easily differentiated. As indicated by its name, the Southeast Asian *P. cocincinus* is of some shade of green dorsally.

The actual shade of green may vary somewhat by population (lizards from one circumscribed area may not be the same shade as those from a distant area), and the color certainly varies

> The babies of both water dragons are lighter in color than adults, and mature males of both develop a jowly look.

The brown water dragon, **Physignathus lesueurii** *(female shown), is becoming a popular pet lizard.*

according to degree of stress (or lack of stress) being felt by the lizard. Stress, as used here, may indicate one or a combination of factors, including, but not necessarily limited to: adverse temperatures, physical restraint, excessive endoparasitism, territorial encroachments by other lizards, or fright. Dominant, sexually active male green water dragons often display the brightest green of all, and may have a yellow or peach suffusion on the throat and anterioventrally. A well-defined vertebral crest extends from nape to about halfway down the lizard's tail. Body bands, when present, are light; tail bands (almost always prominent, especially on the distal two-thirds of the tail) are dark. When dominant males are indulging in territorial displays, the nuchal crest is prominently raised.

With a distribution over much of Southeast Asia, green water dragons are more exclusively tropical, hence more cold-sensitive than their brown cousins. Many of the specimens currently being imported are from Vietnam. These specimens seem to be somewhat darker in coloration and a little smaller than those that used to be imported from Thailand.

The Brown Water Dragon

The second species, *P. lesueuri*, is called either the Australian or the brown water dragon. It, too, is aptly named. It is gray-brown to brown and darkest dorsally, caudally, and on the limbs. Light bands are present on the body and tail; light flecks are present on the limbs. Mature specimens have a suffusion of dark red ventrally. This is brighter on the male than the female, and brightest on sexually active males. Except on the nape, where it is represented by a few rather tall scales, the vertebral crest of the brown water dragon is vestigial. Dorsal and lateral scalation is markedly heterogeneous (includes scales of many varying sizes).

Of the two species of water dragons, the brown is the larger. Occasional males may near 3 feet (0.9 m) in total length. Most are smaller, and females are always smaller. Males of the green water dragon occasionally attain 30 inches (76 cm) in total length. The tail of both species accounts for slightly less than two-thirds of the total length.

If obtained while young, water dragons tame well and usually remain quiet and easily handled as they mature. Although wild-collected adults live well, they often resent familiarity

The hatchlings of both species are very hardy and, if adequately nourished, grow quickly. However, females may not produce viable eggs until their third (or even their fourth) year of life.

Once commonly imported and inexpensive, the Philippine sail-tailed dragon is no longer a common pet trade species.

and frequently injure their noses in attempts to escape. They are seldom as flighty as wild-collected basilisks, however.

It would appear that water dragons are primarily insectivorous in the wild but may consume an occasional small vertebrate and a little fruit and a few flowers as well. In captivity, they readily accept small mice, canned cat food, insects, and some fruits, flowers, and vegetables. Both species are oviparous. Females dig deep nests in which they deposit from 8 to 14 eggs. At 86°F (30°C) the eggs hatch in 72 to 90 days.

Ecologically, water dragons seem to fill much the same niche as green iguanas. Water dragons are most commonly encountered near water while basking on elevated perches. They often choose perches that enable them to drop directly into the water when startled.

In captivity, water dragons prefer sizable cages with a large water receptacle. Ours have done best in walk-in cages in which potted *Ficus* trees provide visual barriers and horizontal limbs at numerous elevations offer ample resting perches. Large containers of clean water are kept in the cages. The dragons often sit or even submerge in these, at times for long periods. Dragons often defecate in their water receptacle, so the water must be changed and the containers scrubbed frequently.

Sail-tailed Dragons

What's a sail-tailed dragon? Since some basilisks truly are "sail-finned" lizards, having prominently raised fins on head, trunk, and tail, and since the members of the genus *Hydrosaurus* have a fin only on their tails, we have always felt the name "sail-tailed" more descriptive than the commonly used name of "sail-finned" dragon. As far as the "dragon" part goes, many Old World lizards are colloquially known as dragons, and since these lizards are quite closely allied to the Old World water dragons (which are known almost everywhere as "dragons"), the common name of sail-tailed dragon seems quite appropriate.

The sail-tailed dragon has a crest along its backbone and a pronounced fin or sail along its tail. The sail-tailed dragons are fairly large in size. As with many lizard species, adult males can be up to 35 percent larger than adult females.

The sail-tails form a genus of two or three species of magnificent agamids. One, the Amboina sail-tailed dragon, *H. amboinensis*, is marginally the world's largest agamid. Adult males of this species may slightly exceed 4 feet (120.8 cm) in length, a measurement most closely approached by some male frilled lizards. Although smaller, the remaining two species of sail-tails, the Philippine, *H. pustulatus*, and the Indonesian, *H. weberi*, also attain impressive sizes. In private and public collections in the United States, neither the Philippine nor the Indonesian sail-tailed dragons are uncommon. The Amboina dragon is rare.

It is as babies to half-grown size that the various hydrosaurs are usually available. As babies to small juveniles, the Philippine species is very inexpensive. Fewer of the Indonesian species are imported, hence those available command a higher price.

As babies, none of the hydrosaurs have the adornment for which they are named. In fact, the sail is still vestigial on half-grown specimens and remains quite low on adult females. It is the adult males that lend credence to the common name of sail-tailed dragon. On the males, the sail rises above the "body of the tail" for at least the diameter of the tail.

None of the sail-tailed dragons are colorful lizards. Babies of the Philippine species are olive tan laterally, often somewhat darker mid-dorsally and with light vertical bars along the side. The adults are darker. Old males can be an unrelieved olive brown.

H. weberi is somewhat dichromatic. Females tend to be olive to olive brown with darker and lighter barring laterally. Males are olive green (lightest anteriorly) with dark barring. *H. weberi* also darkens with advancing age. We have not seen the juveniles of *H. amboinensis*, but the adults we have seen have varied from a boldly reticulated black on olive to a nearly unrelieved olive brown. The females were somewhat lighter than the males. Like many of the big active agamas and iguanids, wild-collected adult hydrosaurs are nervous, and hence are often unsatisfactory captives. They seem unable to adjust to confinement in a cage. If approached (even slowly!) they may dart repeatedly into the sides of their enclosure, injuring their snouts and jaws in the process. This injury results in a reluctance to feed, which leads to the animal's death. On the other hand, babies are relatively quiet and remain that way as they grow.

Hydrosaurs are oviparous. Adult females lay from 4 to 18 eggs. Despite being coveted lizards, few persons or institutions are currently breeding either species. Eggs should be incubated as for the green water dragon, at between 82°F and 86°F (28°C–30°C).

Sail-tailed lizards are quite omnivorous. Besides insects and suitably sized rodents, these lizards will quite readily accept many vegetables and sweet fruits at all stages of their lives.

Bibliography

Demeter, Bela J. 1981. "Captive Maintenance and Breeding of the Chinese Water Dragon, *Physignathus cocincinus*, at the National Zoological Park." Proceedings of the 5th Annual Reptile Symposium on Captive Propagation and Husbandry, Thurmont, MD.

Isham, Steven B. 2007. Anoles "Those Florida Yard Lizards." Commahawk Publishing, Orlando, FL.

Mader, Douglas R. 1994. "Chinese Water Dragons, *Physignathus cocincinus*." Reptiles Magazine 2:1.

Mitchell, Lyndon A. 1985. "Comments on the Maintenance and Reproduction of *Hydrosaurus* pustulatus at the Dallas Zoo." Proceedings of the 9th International Herpetological Symposium on Captive Propagation and Husbandry, Thurmont, MD.

Information and Periodicals

Lizard species that once were rare in the private sector are increasingly available from both private and commercial breeders and importers.

Many sources advertise in the various reptile and amphibian magazines and on the web. A few sources of information and livestock are mentioned below.

Magazines

Reptiles
P.O. Box 6050
Mission Viejo, CA 92690

Herpetological Ecotourism
http://www.amazon-ecotours.com

Web Sites

http://www.kingsnake.com
http://www.mannysreptiles@msn.com
faunaclassifieds.com

Affinity Groups

Herpetological/herpetocultural clubs can be found in many large cities.

Check with the biology department of your nearest university or with the personnel of nature centers or museums to find the club nearest you.

aestivation a period of warm weather inactivity; often triggered by excessive heat or drought

agonistic antagonistic, hostile

allopatric not occurring together but often adjacent

ambient temperature the temperature of the surrounding environment

anterior toward the front

anus the external opening of the cloaca; the vent.

arboreal tree-dwelling

autotomize the ability to break easily, or to voluntarily cast off (and usually to regenerate) a part of the body, such as the tail

bipedally as used here, running on the two hind legs

brumation the reptilian and amphibian equivalent of mammalian hibernation

caudal pertaining to the tail

cb/cb captive-bred, captive-born

cb/ch captive-bred, captive-hatched

chitin the material of which the hard exoskeleton of insects is composed

cloaca the common chamber into which digestive, urinary, and reproductive systems empty and that itself opens exteriorly through the vent or anus

convergent evolution evolution of two unrelated species as the result of environmental conditions

crepuscular active at dusk and/or dawn

deposition as used here, the laying of the eggs

deposition site the spot chosen by the female to lay her eggs or have young

dewlap (also called throat or gular fan) a voluntarily distendable fan of skin on the throats of anoles; these are either missing or comparatively small on females.

dimorphic a difference in form, build, or coloration involving the same species; often sex-linked

diurnal active in the daytime

dorsal pertaining to the back; upper surface

dorsolateral pertaining to the upper sides

dorsum the upper surface

ecological niche the precise habitat utilized by a species

ectothermic cold-blooded

endothermic warm-blooded

form an identifiable species or subspecies

genus a taxonomic classification of a group of species having similar characteristics. The genus falls between the next higher designation of "family" and the next lower designation of "species." "Genera" is the plural of genus. The name of the genus is always capitalized when written.

gravid the reptilian equivalent of mammalian pregnancy

gular pertaining to the throat

heliothermic pertaining to a species that basks in the sun to thermoregulate

hemipenes the dual copulatory organs of male lizards and snakes

hemipenis the singular form of hemipenes

herpetoculture the captive breeding of reptiles and amphibians

herpetoculturist one who indulges in herpetoculture

herpetologist one who indulges in herpetology

herpetology the study (often scientifically oriented) of reptiles and amphibians

hydrate to restore body moisture by drinking or absorption

juvenile a young or immature specimen

labial pertaining to the lips

lateral pertaining to the side

A young adult female northern brown basilisk.

middorsal pertaining to the middle of the back

midventral pertaining to the center of the belly or abdomen

nuchal crest a crest, often voluntarily erectile, on the nape of the neck

oviparous reproducing by means of eggs that hatch after laying

photoperiod the daily/seasonally variable length of the hours of daylight

poikilothermic a species with no internal body temperature regulation

race a subspecies

rostral the (often modified) scale on the tip of the snout

setae the microscopic hairlike bristles in the subdigital lamallae of an anole's toes

species a group of similar creatures that produce viable young when breeding. The taxonomic designation that falls beneath genus and above subspecies. Abbreviation: "sp."

subdigital lamellae the transverse plates (groves and ridges) that extend across the undersurface of an anole's toes

subspecies the subdivision of a species; a race that may differ slightly in color, size, scalation, or other criteria. Abbreviation: "ssp."

sympatric occurring together

taxonomy the science of classification of plants and animals

terrestrial land-dwelling

thermoreceptive sensitive to heat

thermoregulate to regulate (body) temperature by choosing a warmer or cooler environment

thigmothermic Regulating body temperature by basking on or beneath a sun- or otherwise warmed object

vent the external opening of the cloaca; the anus

venter the underside of a creature; the belly

ventral pertaining to the undersurface or belly

ventrolateral pertaining to the sides of the venter (=belly)

vertebral crest (also, middorsal crest) the raised scales, either single or fused, along the middle of the lizard's back